"Two of our greatest needs in the Christian community are to take the need for human transformation seriously and to clarify and demonstrate the sources and methods for that transformation. The unquestioned source is the Holy Spirit. The method is to use all the means of grace possible to yield ourselves completely to the Spirit's power. Here is a very practical guide for Spirit-empowerment."

Dr. Maxie D. Dunnam, President
Asbury Theological Seminary

"Dr. Duewel's pilgrimage in truly making his heart God's home provides a Scripture-documented pattern for those of us who desire God's purity in our lives. Dr. Duewel will expand your mind and knowledge of all of the dimensions of being Spirit-filled."

John E. Mariner, Executive Director
World Witness
The Board of Foreign Missions,
Associate Reformed Presbyterian Church

more
GOD
more power

Filled and Transfigured by the Holy Spirit

Books by Wesley L. Duewel

Ablaze for God
God's Power Is for You
Let God Guide You Daily
Measure Your Life
Mighty Prevailing Prayer
Revival Fire
Touch the World Through Prayer

more
GOD
more power

Filled and Transfigured by the Holy Spirit

Wesley L. Duewel

ZondervanPublishingHouse
Grand Rapids, Michigan

A Division of HarperCollinsPublishers

More God, More Power
Copyright © 2000 by Wesley L. Duewel

Requests for information should be addressed to:

 ZondervanPublishingHouse
Grand Rapids, Michigan 49530

Library of Congress Cataloging-in-Publication Data

Duewel, Wesley L.
　　More God, more power : filled and transformed by the Holy Spirit / Wesley L.
Duewel.
　　　　p.　cm.
　　Includes bibliographical references.
　　ISBN: 0-310-23085-3 (pbk.)
　　1. Holy Spirit.　I. Title.
BT121.2 .D84　2000
231.7—dc21　　　　　　　　　　　　　　　　　　　　　　　　　　99-058136

Interior design by Korina L. Kelley

Printed in the United States of America

---

00 01 02 03 04 05 06 / ❖ DC/ 10 9 8 7 6 5 4 3 2 1

CONTENTS

FOREWORD

Overlooking the mighty Congo River in Kinshasa stands a tall statue of Henry M. Stanley. The famous missionary explorer has his arm extended toward the west with his finger pointing to the vast unchartered regions beyond.

That is what Dr. Wesley Duewel does in these pages. Writing with the passion of an evangelist and the sensitivity of a poet, he lifts his arm and points beyond to the inexhaustible riches of grace still awaiting discovery by every Spirit-filled Christian.

Being cleansed from carnal self-centeredness does not mean that we are completely mature in Christ. Full yieldedness to the Holy Spirit only accelerates the process of becoming more like the Master. We have only begun to fathom the depths of His love. Thanks to the grace of God, as our knowledge of His character and mission grows, and our obedience by faith enlarges to embrace it, the Holy Spirit will continue to fill our lives. Whatever we have realized thus far, the best is yet to be!

What a wonderful message to the saints! How exciting it is to think that we are being transformed into the very image of Jesus, "from glory to glory even as by the Spirit of the Lord" (2 Cor. 3:18 KJV)! While this transfiguration remains ever a vision beyond our experience, it is nevertheless a constant incentive to keep pressing "toward the mark for the prize of the high calling of God in Christ Jesus" (Phil. 3:14 KJV). The closer we get to the heavenly city, the more our soul longs to see His face, and though it does not yet appear what we shall be, we know that when He is revealed, "we shall be like him, for we shall see him as he is" (1 John 3:2).

Reading this book has both inspired and challenged my soul, and I commend it to you with that same expectation.

Dr. Robert E. Coleman
Director, School of World Mission and Evangelism
Trinity Evangelical Divinity School
Deerfield, Illinois

TO YOU, MY READER

This book is written with the conviction that the more God's presence fills you, the more God's power will rest on you, and the more God will make your life a blessing. Although God has wonderful plans for our spiritual lives, far too many Christians never experience the thrill of living for God that Jesus wants them to have. I hope this is not the picture of your life.

My prayer is that this book will open up the spiritual adventure God has planned, prepared, and made possible for you. It starts wherever you are today. And the more you experience and know God, the more He will empower and use you.

Your past may include sins you now regret, wish you could forget, and for which you know you need God's forgiveness before you meet Him in person at your death. Why not ask God for forgiveness today? He will forgive you and make you His child, and you can put all your past sins behind you. Taking that step will open the door into the spiritual adventure God has planned for you. Then you can press on to become more and more like Jesus.

Perhaps you are already a child of God yet some sinful aspects of your nature still hamper your spiritual life. You try to hide and control them, but you know you need a further touch by God before you will feel fully comfortable in His holy presence. You may recognize some hidden spiritual defects, some attitudes you would like to see changed, some areas where you are spiritually weak.

God longs to do further work in your life. Part 1 is especially for you now. Take time today to let God give you deeper, fuller spiritual victory. As surely as God is in heaven, He has Holy Spirit fullness and holy adventure for you. May God help you to find in part 1 the answers you need.

If you are already experiencing such fullness of the Spirit that you can testify that you know God is helping you live in total liberty, spiritual victory, and daily freshness of blessing, then the Holy Spirit longs to open before you the most spiritual and holy adventure you have ever known.

Read part 1 (chapters 1–11) and rejoice that you are now ready to explore the heights and depths of God's rich blessings, holy surprises, and transfiguring grace, which He holds before you as a holy pilgrimage into His likeness. May you find in part 2 many spiritual insights, challenges to fuller Christlikeness, and glimpses of the blessedness to which God calls you as you grow in Christ Jesus.

Plunge into the holy adventure of the Spirit's transfiguring work in your life. Let Him pipe Jesus' love through you to others. Share Jesus' burden for the sins, heartaches, and sorrow of needy people.

May the Holy Spirit fill you and transform you into His likeness, so captivating you with His beauty and glory that you are drawn irresistibly to the pursuit of His holiness and glory. May the Spirit fully captivate your soul and mine and give us as truly a spiritual transfiguration as Christ experienced a physical transfiguration on the mount before Peter, James, and John. (Note that Scripture uses the exact Greek word for our transfiguration [*metamorphoo;* Rom. 12:2; 2 Cor. 3:18] as for Jesus' transfiguration on the mount [Matt. 17:2].)

The Holy Spirit has much more to do in my heart and yours as we come ever closer to God in the Spirit-filled life. Let us worship Him, hunger to be more like Him, and run by grace nearer and nearer until we reach "the whole measure of the fullness of Christ" (Eph. 4:13). Join me in pressing on to take hold of all that for which Christ Jesus took hold of you and me (Phil. 3:12). "Forgetting what is behind and straining toward what is ahead, [let us] press on toward the goal to win the prize for which God has called [us] heavenward in Christ Jesus" (vv. 13–14). May our heart's cry be "More God, more power!"

Wesley L. Duewel

PART 1

Be Filled

CHAPTER 1

You Can Be Filled with the Spirit

What more wonderful news could you, as a Christian, receive from God than that you can be filled with His Spirit? How awesome it is to know that the reason you are where you are spiritually today is that God led you there by His Spirit. How marvelous to realize that the Spirit of God has used you to be a blessing to others or to win a soul to Christ. Yes, every touch of the Spirit of God on your life is wonderful.

Not only can the Spirit of God place His hand on you and use you, He can also fill you. You need not remain satisfied with an occasional awareness of God's Spirit in your life. You can be filled with Him daily, moment by moment. He places the longing for more of His Spirit in your heart because He desires to satisfy you, to amaze you by His abundant answer. Jesus said, "If you then, though you are evil, know how to give good gifts to your children, how much more will your Father in heaven give the Holy Spirit to those who ask him!" (Luke 11:13).

Water is often used in the Bible as a type of the Holy Spirit, while thirst for water is used to illustrate thirst for the Holy Spirit. Envision your soul as a cup that God wants to fill with the Holy Spirit until you can truly say, "My cup overflows" (Ps. 23:5). Perhaps you are as thirsty for more of the Holy Spirit in your life as a thirsty person who pants for water. The psalmist felt that intense longing and wrote, "As the deer pants for streams of water, so my soul pants for you, O God. My soul thirsts for God" (Ps. 42:1–2). God's answer to you is, "'Come! ... Come!' Whoever is thirsty, let him come; and whoever wishes, let him take the free gift of the water of life" (Rev. 22:17). God wants you to have such an abundance of the water of the Spirit that you are more than satisfied. The Spirit's water will spring up within you like a fountain fed by an artesian well (John 4:14). When you are thus filled with the Spirit, it will be impossible to hide the fact, and thirsty people around you will come and be blessed through your life.

Jesus longed for His disciples to be filled with the Spirit. He told them it was necessary for Him to go away so that He could send the Holy Spirit to them (John 16:7). He said that it was better to be Spirit-filled than to be in the company of the incarnate Christ. Jesus also said that the one who prayed in faith would do greater things than He because He was going to the Father and from there would send the Holy Spirit to them (John 14:12; 16:7).

Are you thirsting for more of God's Spirit to fill your life and flow out to others? Hear Jesus: "'If anyone is thirsty, let him come to me and drink. Whoever believes in me, as the Scripture has said, streams of living water will flow from within him.' By this he meant the Spirit, whom those who believed in him were later to receive" (John 7:37–39). If *anyone* is thirsty. That means you. Do you thirst to be greatly used by God? Then this book is for you. You can be abundantly satisfied, filled to overflowing with the Spirit.

More of Your Spirit

More of Your Spirit is my great need—
For this I hunger and for this I plead.
  More of Your presence indwelling me,
  More of Your beauty for all to see,
More of Your blessing in ev'ry way,
More of Your guidance throughout each day!

More of Your Spirit and all His pow'r,
More of His fullness each day and hour,
  More of His triumphant, holy might,
  Complete enduement by day and night,
More of the Spirit's direct supply,
More of the Spirit—for this I cry!

More of Your Spirit's holy fire—
Oh, You know all my deep desire!
  More, ever more of Your glory show,
  More of Shekinah I long to know!

Seal all my ministry now I pray;
Seal with Your glory my life today.

More of Your Spirit is my great need—
For this I hunger and for this plead!
   Oh, pour Your Spirit on me today;
   May He descend on me as I pray!
Oh, how I need Him, yes, ever more;
Fill with Your Spirit, Lord, more and more.

Wesley L. Duewel

Do you know why you so often hunger and thirst to be filled with the Spirit? God created you that way. God created you with a spirit as well as a body so that His Spirit can fill you. You will never be complete until you are Spirit-filled; until then you will have some degree of spiritual restlessness. How wonderful are the love and grace of God that He chose to create you in His own image so that you, His creature, might have fellowship with Him, your Creator. But you are not merely created to have fellowship; you are created to be indwelt with His Holy Spirit.

Even more amazing is that when humans rebel against God, when hearts are so defiled by sin that His Spirit cannot indwell them, God still loves us and longs for us and leaves the way open for anyone to be redeemed from sin. He sent His Son to die to take away our sin, and He sent His Holy Spirit to indwell forgiven sinners, to renew God's image in us so that we can be the temple of the Holy Spirit. Only God's Spirit can make us holy. In the midst of our evil world, God still wills for us to be holy, even as He is holy (1 Peter 1:15–16; 1 John 3:3; 4:17), and that is possible only when His Spirit fills us.

God's will for us is to be filled with His Spirit. "Therefore do not be foolish, but understand what the Lord's will is . . . be filled with the Spirit" (Eph. 5:17–18). "It is God's will that you should be sanctified" (1 Thess. 4:3). The promise is for you (Acts 2:38–39). "May God himself, the God of peace, sanctify you through and through. May your whole spirit, soul and body be kept blameless at the coming of our Lord Jesus Christ. The one who calls you is faithful and he will do it" (1 Thess. 5:23–24).

Does this seem almost too good to be true? Is such an experience for everyone? Yes, indeed, it is God's will for *you*. In fact, it is His command for *you* as decreed in both the Old and New Testaments (Lev. 11:44; 1 Peter 1:15–16). Before you were born, even before the world was created, God planned for you to be Spirit-filled and holy.

No wonder Paul is filled with praise to God. "Praise be to the God and Father of our Lord Jesus Christ, who has blessed us in the heavenly realms with every spiritual blessing in Christ. For he chose us in him before the creation of the world to be holy and blameless in his sight" (Eph. 1:3–4). Christ reconciled you by His "physical body through death to present you holy in his sight, without blemish and free from accusation" (Col. 1:22). Perhaps you reply that this will be true in heaven. Of course it will. But it will begin down here, or it will never be true in heaven for you. "[God] has raised up a horn of salvation for us . . . to remember . . . the oath he swore to our father Abraham; to rescue us from the hand of our enemies, and to enable us to serve him without fear in holiness and righteousness before him all our days" (Luke 1:69–75).

We cannot be loyal to the heart of God the Father, to the shed blood of God the Son, or to the ministry of God the Holy Spirit unless we obtain, live, and proclaim this full and free salvation—a Spirit-filled, holy life. We dishonor and slander the holy God if we suggest that He is pleased to dwell in an unholy heart that has an unsurrendered will. Since He loves us so infinitely and longs for us so constantly, how could He be satisfied with incomplete surrender and incomplete victory for anyone who loves Him? Are not the grace, power, and love of God adequate to meet the need of anyone? Can they not meet your need? Yes, thank God, they can.

God Can Perform His Word

Our God has given His command
    That we should holy be;
Then cannot His almighty hand
    Give us His purity?
He will not give command to us
    For what we cannot know.
He can impart His holiness
    Till we His likeness show.

Our God has promised in His Word
    That we can be made clean.
No idle word from Him is heard;
    His promise will be seen.
He will perform His full intent

And purify us here.
His Holy Spirit He has sent
    To cleanse and bring us near.

God will His Spirit to you give
    To cleanse you and empow'r.
You need Him so that you can live
    A holy life each hour.
His promise is "to all afar"
    Who shall His Word receive.
Lord, we today Your children are;
    Your promise we believe.

Make us all pure till we become
    Our Savior's spotless bride,
Till we into His beauty come
    And stand our Lord beside.
The beauty of Your holiness
    Upon our lives bestow,
Till we by You in bridal dress
    Will all Your glory show.

Wesley L. Duewel

CHAPTER 2

This Is Your Greatest Need

Spirit-filled people are the church's greatest need today. The church has forsaken its first love (Rev. 2:4) and has lost its first power. As a result, it has largely lost its miraculous growth rate. Of few places can it be said today that the Lord is adding to the church daily those being saved (Acts 2:47). The church of our generation is facing a greater opportunity, a greater need, and a greater challenge than the church of any previous generation. But how largely God's glory has departed from our churches. Just as Israel lost the glory of God's presence (1 Sam. 4:21), so *Ichabod* ("the glory has departed") can be written over the door of many places of worship today.

Our secular, materialistic age has lost God-consciousness. If this world is to be saved from the impending judgment of God and escape the chaos of self-destruction, we must be humbled before God. Our generation will come to God only when it sees new demonstrations of God's reality, presence, and power in His people individually and as the church. Therefore, the church must be revived. We must have a new visitation of God.

The responsibility of the church in our generation is greater than that in any previous age. Earth's population is multiplying rapidly, and more millions are waiting to be reached with the message of Christ than ever before. Millions today are militantly anti-God. Never before in human history has atheism had the backing of organized government as it has had in communism. The blood of a larger unreached world is upon the church today more than ever before (Ezek. 3:18).

The church has never been faced with such tremendous opportunity as it faces now. Never has such a large percentage of the world's population been able to read and write as today—and literacy continues to increase rapidly. Thus more people than ever can read the Word and Christian literature for themselves. Never has it been possible for the Christian witness to reach so many areas of the earth so quickly and conveniently as today. Television, radio, and the world wide web blanket the globe. Audio-visual aids such as slides, films, video, and even television are available for evangelistic use as never before.

Thank God for millions of true children of God around the world. Thank God for every church and organization that effectively preaches the Gospel of Jesus Christ. But although the church can be found in more places than ever before, it is largely asleep—lukewarm, lifeless, powerless. We are not impacting our generation as the early church, although few in number, impacted the people of its time.

Where must revival begin? It can come only through those who already know the transforming power of Jesus Christ. Revival can come only from God and only through His people (2 Chron. 7:14). Is your local church experiencing continuous revival today? Are you? The church reflects its individual members—you and me.

The church will be ablaze for God only when you and I are ablaze for Him. The church will be as mighty for God as you and I are mighty for God. The church will be no more Spirit-filled than you and I are Spirit-filled. We have all read the account of the early church in the Acts of the Apostles. Is God not the same today? We have more godly examples to stir us to faith than the early church had. We know more about what revival can mean than the first-century apostles knew. We have many times more praying people today than the early church had. We have more unanswered prayers stored in heaven, just waiting for us to claim and release in holy power, than any previous generation of Christians (Rev. 8:1–5). If the apostles were privileged to reap the labors of those before them (John 4:38), think what tremendous labors and prayers we are privileged to reap in our twenty-first century.

What is the difference? Are not God's promises for us today? Is this not still the dispensation of the Holy Spirit? Did not God promise to pour out His Spirit in the last days upon all people? Yes, "'In the last days,' God says, 'I will pour out my Spirit on all people'" (Acts 2:17). Human need is just the same as or greater than ever before. God is just the same as He has always been. What is the difference?

There can be but one answer. Although more people profess to be Christian than ever before, our knowledge of theology is greater than that of the early church, and we have more recorded examples of the Spirit's mighty working in Christian biography and history than the early church ever dreamed, we do not have as much of the presence and power of God. We are not as filled with the Spirit as God longs for us to be.

There is but one prayer that we can pray for the church: "Lord, send a revival and begin it in me. Come upon Your church again in all Your power. Send Your Shekinah glory into our midst again." And there is but one hunger that must fill your heart and mine above all we have ever known: "Lord, fill me more and more with Your Spirit. Fill me more with Your Spirit than I have ever known before."

No matter what experience of God's grace you may have known, you need more of the Holy Spirit. If you have never yet experienced the infilling of the Holy Spirit, this is your greatest need. If you have had the gracious experience of a definite crisis cleansing of your heart and enduement with God's Spirit, even so, your need is for more of the Holy Spirit. This book has a message for you. Will you keep your heart open to all God wants to say to you? Standing one day beside a rushing, flooded river as it neared the ocean, I wrote the following words of prayer.

Sweep, Mighty Flood!

Lord, send revival in mighty flood-tide;
Send streams of blessing to sweep far and wide.
    Send them engulfing like waves of the sea;
    Sweep through our lowlands and work mightily.

Send the outpourings of God's holy rain
Send mighty cloud-bursts again and again.
    Strike holy lightning at home and abroad;
    Speak in Your thunder, O Spirit of God!

Fill all our churches with rivers of pow'r;
Flood man's embankments in this holy hour!
Sweep away rubbish and all the debris;
Sweep all the hindrances out to the sea.

Things long unmoved by our normal smooth way
You can remove by Your flood-tide's full sway.
Unsightly jumble that littered each side
Sweep to obliv'on by Your holy tide.

Lord, send revival to flood all around;
Flood by Your blessing all low, parched ground.
Sweep on in power; oh, sweep, mighty flood!
Sweep in all fullness, O river of God!

Wesley L. Duewel

CHAPTER 3

The Word Pictures God Uses

God's work in our soul is so glorious that Scripture uses many terms, word pictures, and illustrations to describe it. One cannot preach the whole Gospel by using exclusively any one of these many terms, for the wholeness of the Gospel consists in the balanced use of them all.

Human language and experience are finite, even as we have a finite body and spirit. But our finite spirit is related to the infinite Spirit of God since we are created in God's image (Gen. 1:27). No conflict exists between the infinite and the finite; the finite is based on and dependent on the infinite. When the infinite Spirit of God indwells, possesses, and works in our finite soul, that work of God partakes of the greatness, glory, and infinity of God. No one human word adequately expresses God's work in our soul, and no human illustration adequately explains it.

God the Holy Spirit uses a variety of words and pictures to describe the new birth, the first great work of God in us. It is called the forgiveness of sins (Acts 10:43) and the passing from death to life (1 John 3:14), from darkness to light (Eph. 5:8), and from the power of Satan to God (Acts 26:18). It is being born of God (1 John 5:4) and of the Spirit (John 3:5–6), being made alive with Christ (Col. 2:13), and it is called salvation (Acts 4:12). It involves being justified by faith (Rom. 3:28), being adopted into God's family (Eph. 1:5), having our sins blotted out (Isa. 43:25) or removed from us as far as the east is from the west (Ps. 103:12), and receiving peace with God (Rom. 5:1) and the testimony of the Spirit that we are children of God (Rom. 8:16). It is being made alive spiritually (Eph.

2:5), regenerated (born again, Titus 3:5), washed from our sins (Rev. 22:14), pardoned (Mic. 7:18), and delivered from darkness.

Similarly, God has used a variety of words and pictures to describe the sinful nature (Rom. 8:5) with which we are born, the nature we inherit from Adam because of his sin. People have referred to it as original sin, our Adamic nature, or simply carnality. The Bible calls it our old self (6:6), the old man, the law of sin and death (8:2), the sinful nature (8:5), the flesh, the carnal mind, the sinful mind (v. 7; in the English "flesh" is also used for the flesh of the body), sin (in the singular as distinguished from "sins" in the plural), the body of sin (6:6), and the law of sin (7:23).

The Bible teaches that in the heart of the born-again child of God there remains this sinful condition with which every human being is born. The forgiveness of sins, regenerating work of the Spirit, and justifying action of Christ deliver us from the guilt and penalty of sin but not from the indwelling nature of sin.

The newborn Christian is born of the Spirit but is not filled with the Spirit until he or she asks and receives. The Bible teaches that there is a great crisis commitment of our souls, a deeper, higher, cleansing work of the Holy Spirit in our hearts as believers. Scripture is also lavish in the multitude of expressive terms and pictures used to describe this. Again, all are helpful, but no one term or illustration is adequate in itself. God is greater than all His attributes, and being filled with the Spirit is greater than all the Bible terms used for it.

Gestalt psychology has taught us that the whole is always greater than the sum of its parts. The famous six blind men of India who went to examine an elephant each touched a separate part of the animal. Each insisted that he now knew from personal experience what an elephant was like. But the one who grabbed the tail thought the elephant was like a rope, and the one who got his arms around the elephant's leg thought it was like a tree. The one who felt the elephant's side insisted the elephant was like a wall, while the one who grabbed the trunk of the elephant was equally sure the elephant was like a snake. Each had a part of true knowledge, each was sure he had the last word, yet how lacking in total understanding was each man.

These men are like some sincere but misguided children of God who argue over shibboleths and various aspects of divine truth. God is greater than all the words we can use to describe Him. He has condescended to reveal Himself to us, and this is possible only because humans are personal even as God is personal. We can understand Him through the terms we know and the experiences we have shared. Solomon recognized that no temple could contain all of God, yet God could indwell the temple (1 Kings 8:27). Anything that God is or does is greater than our power to describe it. No human description is adequate to portray the fullness of divine reality. Words do illuminate our hearts and minds, bless our souls, and help us to understand, but we must remember their limitations.

How misguided some sincere children of God have been as they have argued over terms and illustrations for God's work in our souls. How many unholy arguments there have been over the doctrine and experience of holiness. Because God realizes far better than we do how limited our human words and experiences are, He is lavish in the terms and pictures He gives us. To overemphasize or to neglect any is to lack the wholeness of divine revelation, placing us in danger of inadequate personal experience of the grace of God, unsound doctrine, and incomplete presentation of the Gospel.

This subsequent Christian experience has been called many names by Bible teachers: the deeper life, the victorious life, the higher life, the surrendered life, absolute surrender, the life of full surrender, the life of full consecration, the quiet life, the crucified life, the rest of faith, the second blessing (this is perhaps one of the most unfortunate of terms, since there are thousands of blessings in the Christian life, and this great work of the Holy Spirit is far more than a blessing), and others.

Many biblical terms are used to describe the glorious experience provided by Christ's death. Study the references that follow, noting how this doctrine is found again and again in God's Word. The Holy Spirit strives to emphasize the urgency for each child of God to experience God's grace.

> *Cleansing from all sin:* Individual "sins"—always in the plural—are forgiven, but the source, or sin nature—always in the singular (1 John 1:7)—must be cleansed. Our sins can be forgiven; our sinful nature can be cleansed.

> *Crucified with Christ:* Rom. 6:6; Gal. 2:20; i.e., so that the life of the carnal self, the sinful nature, is dead (Rom. 6:11).

> *Baptized with the Holy Spirit:* Matt. 3:11; Acts 1:5; 11:16.

> *Filled with the Holy Spirit:* Acts 2:4; 4:31; 13:52; Eph. 5:18. This results in a person being "full" of the Holy Spirit (Acts

6:3, 5, 8; 7:55; 11:24). A person can be filled with all the fullness of God (Eph. 3:19; 4:13).

Holiness: Rom. 6:19, 22; 2 Cor. 7:1; Eph. 4:24; 1 Thess. 3:13; 4:7; Heb. 12:14. Compare also the use of "holy"—Rom. 12:1; Eph. 1:4; 5:27; Col. 1:22; 3:12; 1 Peter 1:15–16; 2:5; 2 Peter 3:11.

Entire sanctification: "Sanctify you through and through" (1 Thess. 5:23).

Other Scriptures on sanctification: John 17:17, 19; Acts 20:32; 26:18; 1 Cor. 1:30; Eph. 5:26; 1 Thess. 4:3; 5:23; 2 Tim. 2:21; Heb. 2:11; 10:10, 14; 1 Peter 1:2.

Purified, pure heart: Ps. 51:2, 7, 10; Ezek. 36:25–26; Acts 15:9; 2 Cor. 7:1; Eph. 5:26; Titus 2:14; James 4:8; 1 Peter 1:22; 1 John 1:7, 9; 3:3.

Perfection: Heb. 10:14. Compare Matt. 5:48; 2 Cor. 13:9, 11; Eph. 4:12–13; Col. 1:28; Heb. 12:23. We are never perfect in mind or actions, but we can be made perfect in love— 1 John 2:5; 4:12, 17–18.

Being filled with the Spirit means dying to self in order to receive an abundant spiritual life. It is circumcision of the heart and crucifixion of the old self. It is being baptized with the Holy Spirit and fire. It is sweeping the soul clean and rooting out all bitterness. It is cleansing from all sin and perfecting in love. All are gloriously true, yet the experience of God's gracious work is greater than all the terms and pictures put together. Human language cannot adequately portray the greatness of God's work.

Preaching this experience as primarily the doctrine of any particular church, organization, or person is wrong. Let us not build our theological arguments with the prestige of human names, but rather on Scripture and in the words of Scripture. John Wesley declared that the exact term used was not the main issue.[1] He said, "Avoid all magnificent and pompous words; indeed you need give it no general name—neither perfection, sanctification, nor the second blessing."[2] Let people call God's wondrous grace by any scriptural term they will; let it be our chief concern to preach it, live it, and manifest it so clearly and winsomely that others hunger to obtain the Spirit's fullness, freedom, and deliverance.

I have chosen "Spirit-filled" because I fear there is a danger of emphasizing any experience, whether of the new birth or of sanctification, as "it" more than we emphasize God, the source. We are in danger of glorying more in "it" than in Him, of resting our faith on an experience of God's grace rather than on Him. The term "Spirit-filled life" puts emphasis on the Holy Spirit and His relationship to us. There is no holiness apart from Him.

The Spirit-Filled Life

Oh the Spirit-filled life! is it thine? is it thine?
Is thy soul wholly filled with the Spirit divine?
    O thou child of the King, has He fallen on thee?
    Does He reign in thy soul, so that all men may see
    The dear Saviour's blest image reflected in thee?

Has He swept through thy soul like the waves of the sea?
Does the Spirit of God daily rest upon thee?
    Does He sweeten thy life, does He keep thee from care?
    Does He guide thee and bless thee in answer to prayer?
    Is it joy to be led of the Lord anywhere?

Is He near thee each hour, does He stand at thy side?
Does He gird thee with strength, has He come to abide?
    Does He give thee to know that all things may be done
    Through the grace and the power of the Crucified One?
    Does He witness to thee of the glorified Son?

Has He purged thee of dross with the fire from above?
Is He first in thy thoughts, has He all of thy love?
    Is His service thy choice, and is sacrifice sweet?
    Is the doing His will both thy drink and thy meat?
    Dost thou run at His bidding with glad eager feet?

Has He freed thee from self and from all of thy greed?
Dost thou hasten to succor thy brother in need?
    As a soldier of Christ dost thou hardness endure?
    Is thy hope in the Lord everlasting and sure?
    Hast thou patience and meekness, art tender and pure?

Oh, the Spirit-filled life may be thine, may be thine,
In thy soul evermore the Shekinah may shine;
    It is thine to live with the tempests all stilled,
    It is thine with the blessed Holy Ghost to be filled;
    It is thine, even thine, for thy Lord has so willed.

George B. Kulp

CHAPTER 4

God: The Source of the Spirit-Filled Life

Humankind has largely forgotten God. Never have we been more conscious of power than in this atomic age, but we have almost forgotten the almighty power of God. People have little reverence for God. Even many Christians speak of God in too casual and familiar a way. We have forgotten what it means for God to be holy. God announced to Moses, "I, the LORD your God, am holy" (Lev. 19:2). Since this holy God is the source of the Spirit-filled life, the chief characteristics of the Spirit-filled life are God's holiness and power.

The Hebrew word *qodesh* means separateness, holiness, soundness. That which is holy is set apart for God and is sacred to God. A holy person is separated from sin and separated to God. He or she is pure as Jesus is pure (1 John 3:3). Some Bible translations use "holy" and some use "sacred" to translate the word that means set apart for God.

Have you ever caught a vision of the holiness of God? Few catch this vision of God as He longs for them to do. In the Old Testament the place where God met with man was called holy ground (Ex. 3:5). God's temple was holy (Ps. 5:7). In it were a Holy Place and a Most Holy Place, where God revealed Himself (Ex. 26:33). Everything related to the Old Testament worship of God was termed "holy," for example, holy furnishings (1 Kings 8:4) and the "most holy" altar (Ex. 29:37).

Strict laws governed approaching such a holy God. The priests wore holy garments (Ex. 28:2) and were anointed with holy anointing oil (30:25), holy perfume (v. 36), and holy water

(Num. 5:17). They offered holy gifts (Ex. 28:38). The ark was holy (2 Chron. 35:3) and so was the tithe (Lev. 27:30). Prophets were termed holy (Luke 1:70) even as the New Testament apostles were termed holy (Eph. 3:5). The Sabbath was a holy day (Ex. 16:23), and on it God's worshipers were to be holy (Lev. 20:7–8) and were to worship God in the splendor of His holiness (1 Chron. 16:29).

Everything about God is called holy. His holy covenant (Luke 1:72) and holy promises (Ps. 105:42) were recorded in His holy Scriptures (Rom. 1:2) by holy writers who were carried along by the Holy Spirit (2 Peter 1:21). God dwells in a holy heaven (Ps. 20:6) and sits on a holy throne (Ps. 47:8), where He is served by holy angels (Mark 8:38). Twenty-five times the Bible says that God's name is holy; fifty-one times He is called "the Holy One of Israel."

God the Father is called the Holy Father (John 17:11), God the Son is called God's holy servant (Acts 4:27), and the Holy Spirit is repeatedly (at least eighty-three times) called holy. Day and night as the blessed Trinity is worshiped in heaven, the seraphim (Isa. 6:3) and other heavenly beings (Rev. 4:8) cry in reverent worship and loving adoration, "Holy, holy, holy." The Bible emphasizes the holiness of God more than any other attribute, even more than His love. His holiness is the source of all His other attributes.

God's holiness is further symbolized by the holy fire that is so often pictured as surrounding Him or proceeding from Him (Heb. 12:29: "our God is a consuming fire"). God first revealed Himself to Moses in fire (Ex. 3:2), and He descended at Sinai in holy fire (19:18). The sight of the glory of the Lord on Sinai was like "consuming fire" (24:16–17). The mountain "blazed with fire to the very heavens" (Deut. 4:11), and God spoke out of the midst of the fire (v. 12). When the people saw and heard, they trembled with fear and stayed at a distance (Ex. 20:18). God's throne is flaming with fire (Dan. 7:9), and a river of fire flows from before Him (v. 10). Seven lamps of fire blaze before God's throne (Rev. 4:5) as does a sea of glass mixed with fire (15:2).

When Moses spent forty days in the presence of this holy God, even the skin of his face began to glow and others feared to draw near him (Ex. 34:29–35). When Isaiah caught a vision of the holiness of God, he called out, "Woe to me! . . . I am ruined! For I am a man of unclean lips" (Isa. 6:5). Even the holy prophet felt his unholiness before God! As soon as Ezekiel saw the holy God with fire proceeding from Him, he fell facedown (Ezek. 1:26–28). Daniel saw in a vision God's flaming face and eyes and fell helpless with his face to the ground (Dan. 8:17–18). When Peter saw Christ's holy power, he fell at Jesus' knees, saying, "Go away from me, Lord; I am a sinful man!" (Luke 5:8). When Christ was transfigured by glory, His disciples fell on their faces before Him (Matt. 17:6). When Saul caught the vision of Christ, he fell blind to the earth (Acts 9:3–4). Even John, the beloved disciple who pillowed his head on Jesus' breast, when he caught a sight of the holy glory of Christ with His flaming eyes and glowing feet, fell at Jesus' feet as though dead (Rev. 1:13–17).

Who is that presumptuous person who wants to stand bolt upright before such a holy God and insist that God does not really intend for humans to be holy? Seven times in the Bible God says, "I am holy," and each time He adds, "Be holy." Who is that person who presumes he can keep his own stubborn will and insist on his own way, cling to his own sinful nature, and still want to be filled with the Holy Spirit?

Will such a sovereign, holy God tolerate sin to reign unchallenged in the heart of any child of His? The God of the Bible must provide a redemption adequate to destroy the works of the devil (1 John 3:8). Such a perfect God cannot provide anything less than a perfect redemption. He cannot be content unless He perfects holiness in every obedient child of His (2 Cor. 7:1). The great Creator who made us in His own image of holiness cannot do less than provide a redemption that cleanses us from all sin. He will never concede defeat to Satan and permit sin to be the norm in the life of the obedient Christian.

Will God provide the miracle of the new birth but provide nothing to deal with the sinful nature, that carnality that is hostile and does not submit to God's law and never can (Rom. 8:7)? Will the God, whose name is Jealous (Ex. 34:14; Deut. 4:24), be satisfied with the partial affection of our divided heart, permitting us to keep longings for the world without cleansing them away for us? No! He will command us to love Him with all our heart, mind, soul, and strength (Deut. 6:5; Matt. 22:37–38). Will the God who is light and in whom is no darkness at all (1 John 1:5) indwell a soul and be satisfied to leave in that soul areas of darkness, sin, and uncleanness? A thousand times no! Let God be true though every man be proved a liar!

If holiness is Christlikeness, we dare not think of holiness as a mere label, a nominal term. Christ loved the church and gave Himself for it to sanctify and cleanse it. Will He be satisfied to let it remain spotted by carnality, dressed in garments stained by the sinful nature (2 Peter 3:14)? Never! It is libel against God the Father, God the Son, and God the Holy Spirit to deny that when God fills us with Himself He cleanses us from all sin. When God empowers us, He enables us to fulfill His commands and to be holy before Him all the days of our life (Luke 1:75). The purpose of Calvary was to completely meet our spiritual need. God the Son would not have died outside the city gate for a sanctification for us (Heb. 13:12) that was a mere shibboleth, a partial salvation with nothing but nominal cleansing.

The sinful state of the carnal soul is an abomination in God's holy sight. When we refuse to accept His cleansing grace, we insult His holy love. Every excuse we make for retaining our own stubborn will is a defiance of God's holy will, a slander on God's character. May He cleanse us from all sin (Eph. 5:25–27)!

His Likeness I Shall Share

Can Satan so my spirit chain
  That Christ cannot set free?
Can evil so my nature stain
  Till pure I cannot be?
My sinful nature in me dwells
  And brings forth bitterness.
Can Christ not dig salvation's wells
  And fill with holiness?

How stubborn often is my will!
  Can Christ not this subdue?
Can He not yieldedness instill
  And save me through and through?
Evil affections often rise
  And burn with wrong desire.
I know in Christ deliverance lies;
  He baptizes with fire!

Say not the devil's work has gone
    Too deep for Christ to heal!
Say not I can but struggle on,
    Nor Calv'ry's triumph feel!
Though evil in my spirit reign,
    My Lord is Conqueror.
He shall His great desire attain
    And prove Himself Victor.

Though I am but a mortal man
    My soul was made for God.
He Who in me His work began
    Will cleanse me with His blood.
He will in me His work complete
    Till I His image bear.
My Christ can never know defeat;
    Till I His likeness share!

Wesley L. Duewel

CHAPTER 5

Human Beings: The Beings to Be Spirit-Filled

Have you ever understood the wonder of God's creating us in His own image (Gen. 1:26–27)? God's purpose was to create us as moral beings with whom He could fellowship and in whom He could dwell. Thus, it was necessary for God to create human beings with a finite personal spirit, for God is Himself infinite personal Spirit. God can only indwell us because both He and we are personal spirit beings. We were created to be Spirit-filled, to be holy, and to be in holy fellowship with the holy God. What amazing love! And because we were created to be Spirit-filled, we can never be spiritually satisfied until we are Spirit-filled.

My God Has Made My Heart His Home

Will He Who earth and heaven fills
　　Indwell this humble heart of mine?
Behold! the great Creator wills
　　To live in me His life divine!

Will He the King and Lord of all,
　　The Sovereign, the All-glorious One,
Claim home within my heart so small,
　　I who am worthless and undone?

Will He rejoice to share my heart?
　　Will He show such love unto me?
Then let me give Him every part
　　With all I am and e'er can be.

Then let Him cleanse me through and through;
  Then let Him for Himself prepare.
Let Him transform my heart anew
  And fill with heaven's beauty rare.

Then let my God have His own way
  And do in me whate'er He will.
My all I place beneath His sway
  That He may all my being fill.

Come, Holy Father, Holy Son,
  Come, Holy Spirit, live in me.
O ever-blessed Three-in-One,
  Make me Your home eternally.

Amazing love, how can it be
  That God should stoop to me to come!
Amazing love to me, to me!
  My God has made my heart His home!

Wesley L. Duewel

Holiness is original only in God; human holiness is derived from God. Just as love is not a material substance, there is no material "thing" called "holiness." Holiness is the holy nature of God alone, and humans have holiness only when they are indwelt by the holy God. Holiness in humans is not some kind of spiritual degree or diploma to be attained. God did not put some "holiness" in Adam when He created him and then remove that "holiness" when man sinned.

When God created Adam, He gave him a "spirit" so he could be indwelt by the Holy Spirit. From the moment of Adam's creation and God's breathing into him, Adam was indwelt by the Holy Spirit. He was innocent and pure but had no maturity of holy character, for character is developed in the way God ordained, by our choosing obedience to God's will and refusing temptation. Adam could have quickly developed holy maturity of character, but when Adam sinned, he sinned God's holy indwelling presence out of his life and thus was no longer holy. He was guilty and void of God's holy presence. The only holiness anyone ever has is the presence of the holy God living within so that God expresses His holiness through that person's finite spirit. When the Holy Spirit leaves, a person has nothing but an empty spirit.

When sin expels the Holy Spirit from one's heart, the Holy Spirit leaves, but sin remains as a state of our being. We are both guilty and unclean. We sense both the guilt and the power of sin, for we have become a slave to sin. Holiness is like light, which becomes darkness the moment the source of light is removed. Thus, holiness is not possessed apart from the indwelling of the Holy Spirit.

When Adam sinned, he sided with Satan against God. The Holy Spirit was no longer Lord in Adam's life and ceased to indwell him. Instantly Adam was deprived of God's holy presence, and thus he became depraved. Deprived of the Holy Spirit in the presence of the evil tempter, Adam quickly succumbed to Satan and became increasingly more depraved. Evil persons always become worse and worse, deceiving and being deceived (2 Tim. 3:13). Sin develops sinful character and makes a person more and more weakened by sin, blinded by sin, and enslaved to sin. No sinner is ever delivered from sin except by the mighty power of God.

But how is a person indwelt by sin? Is it not in some sense an indwelling by Satan? Note how Satan counterfeits and imitates God. He is the god of this world, of sinners. A sinner is as truly a child of the devil as a believer is a child of God. Just as the newborn soul is to a degree indwelt by the Holy Spirit (for anyone who does not have the Spirit of Christ does not belong to Christ—Rom. 8:9), the child of the devil is to a degree indwelt by Satan or one of his sinful spirits, though he is not demon possessed or controlled. Satan prostitutes a person's personality, which was meant to be indwelt by the Holy Spirit.

The Shame Of Carnality

Oh tragic shame! Oh deep disgrace
   That man who once God's image bore
Has chosen sin, fled from God's face,
   Become defiled yet more and more!
Behold what privilege man lost—
   The presence of indwelling God.
To fill with God once more, what cost!
   The Son of God's own precious blood!

Behold mankind once pure and free
   Now fettered by the chains of sin!

Behold what depths of misery,
  With Satan's image stamped within!
Man made to be the home of God
  Is now unclean, depraved, and vile.
Satan has shed his sin abroad
  To weaken, darken, and defile.

Where once God's image could be seen
  Satanic likeness now is borne.
Where purity dwelt, man unclean
  Is empty-hearted, lost, forlorn.
The sinful works of carnal self
  Are manifested everywhere
And of all Satan's evil wealth
  Mankind, alas, has his full share.

O soul of mine, you were depraved,
  You were by self and evil filled.
You would be lost had Christ not saved
  And full redemption freely willed.
Flee to the cross, plunge 'neath Christ's blood;
  'Tis there alone you can be clean.
Be freed from sin and filled with God
  Till His own image can be seen.

It would be shame to hesitate
  When Christ was crucified for you.
Don't grieve Him, or His will debate;
  Be crucified with Him anew.
Appropriate all He provides—
  Indwelling power and purity
Till God Triune in you resides
  And men in you God's image see.

Wesley L. Duewel

CHAPTER 6

The Deeper, Surrendered Life

God has a deeper experience for each Christian, a life of full surrender in which the Holy Spirit is Lord of one's life. I call it the Spirit-filled life. Likewise, Satan has a deeper experience of defilement for the sinner, a work of evil in which the sinner is not merely a child of the devil but is demon possessed. Satan is not omnipresent; hence, he makes use of evil spirits, and demon possession is when Satan indwelling a person through an evil spirit is lord of the life.

The condition for entering the Spirit-filled life is an act of absolute surrender to God's will and to the infilling of the Holy Spirit. The condition for entering a demon-possessed life is an act of absolute surrender to Satan. The condition for continuous infilling of the Holy Spirit and a life of holiness is continuous obedience and surrender to the Holy Spirit. The condition for continuous demon possession is continuous obedience and surrender to Satan.

An act of the will, deliberately turning away from God to sin, can deprive one of the Holy Spirit. An act of the will, deliberately turning away from Satan through the grace of God and the power of the Holy Spirit, can bring deliverance from demon possession. I have seen the name of Jesus cast out a demon in a mere moment of time. I have also seen a temporary surrender to the will of God, coupled with the power of Jesus' name, cast out the demon, but then I have seen that same person again become demon possessed. Those of us who were dealing with this person recognized that in each instance the new demon convulsion came when the person lied to the Holy Spirit or compromised with a false religion. After this had happened several times, the person finally confessed, "You keep casting out the demon, but I keep inviting him back in." Just as truly as a person can pray, "Come into my heart, Lord Jesus," a person can open himself or herself for an evil spirit to enter. It is an act of surrender of the will.

Overemphasis on Satan and the demonic is always a potential danger. Satan is evil and powerful, but he is a limited being. He is not parallel to God. Rather, he is a created angel who sinned and who cannot go beyond the limits God has set for him. He was defeated at Calvary and knows he is destined for the lake of burning fire and sulfur (Rev. 20:10). His demons know they have the same destination and fear God and the Christian's prayer (Matt. 8:29; Luke 8:31; James 4:7).

Satan wants us to get our eyes on him rather than on God. Some people are more Satan-conscious than God-conscious. This is spiritually unwise, because it causes one to fear. Christ repeatedly told His disciples to "fear not." Focusing on Satan robs a person of joy, blessing, and spiritual liberty.

The demonic is real just as sin is real, but Christ defeated Satan at Calvary. You don't have to defeat him, because Jesus already did. And Jesus has also given you authority over Satan and his demons (Luke 10:19). Sin can be cleansed from your life because Christ has overcoming spiritual victory for you. Rejoice in Him. Glory in His victory. You don't need to tremble before Satan. Christ in you is greater than all the power of the enemy (1 John 4:4).

After I had spent hours of fasting and prayer to no avail with one demon-possessed person, a nominal Christian, he finally turned and said to me, "There is no use in your praying for me. You might just as well stop. I sold myself to Satan. I promised him I would do anything he wanted me to do!" I pled with him and begged him to renounce Satan and surrender to Christ, but he refused. His father was a minister, but the demon-possessed youth had trifled with a non-Christian religion. At times during demon attacks he became almost bestial and was obscene and vile in speech. Suddenly he died, with no apparent physical cause. He seemed to have died of demon possession. Satan took him. Alas, too few of God's children are really filled with the Holy Spirit. And thank God that comparatively few of Satan's children are demon possessed, except in nations where Satan and demons are worshiped.

The fall (Adam's choice of sin) destroyed the moral image of God in human beings. Adam became unholy and sinful. To this day, flesh gives birth to flesh (John 3:6). But the fall did not destroy our personality, our spirit nature. You and I are still the same order of being in our spirit nature as God. No other earthly creation is spirit but humans. Humankind is therefore still redeemable and capable of being indwelt by God. If anyone will open the door, Christ will come in (Rev. 3:20). Anyone who does not have the Spirit of Christ does not belong to Christ (Rom. 8:9).

Then what does the Scripture mean when Jesus says of the Holy Spirit, "He lives with you and will be in you" (John 14:17)? The Bible clearly indicates degrees of indwelling, of relationship with God. God through His omnipotence and omnipresence indwells the whole world (Acts 17:28). But from the standpoint of spiritual relationship, He indwells only the born-again child of God as Father, Teacher, Witness, and Guide. The Spirit bears testimony in the heart of every child of God (Rom. 8:16; 1 John 5:10). Those who are cleansed and sanctified by the Spirit following a crisis of full surrender know a new fullness of the indwelling of the Spirit. Only they are truly filled with the Spirit as Lord. There is a difference in having the indwelling Spirit and in being filled with the Spirit, that is, in experiencing His lordship.

The lordship of the indwelling Spirit permits a new communion of His will with ours as His will indwells and energizes our spirit, as His loving, holy nature expresses itself through our spirit. He pours the love of God into our heart (Rom. 5:5), flooding us with His love. From within our innermost being streams of living water flow (John 7:38), rivers of all the fruit of the Spirit—love, joy, peace, patience, kindness, goodness, faithfulness, gentleness, and self-control (Gal. 5:22–23). Spirit-filled persons not only have deep spiritual joy, they joy in the Holy Spirit (Acts 13:52; Rom. 14:17; 15:13).

In the unique mystery of Christ's incarnation, the divine and human natures of Christ unite but result not in a dual personality but in a communion of natures. In a lesser but wonderfully real sense, when a person is Spirit-filled, the whole Trinity indwells that person through the Holy Spirit. It is not an incarnation, but it is a gloriously real indwelling. There is no resulting duality of persons in the Spirit-filled believer, but a uniting of personality under the lordship of the Holy Spirit (Ps. 86:11).

No sinner can ever be satisfied by the pleasures of this world, because God created people with the spiritual capacity to be indwelt by the Spirit of God. We will never be satisfied until we are indwelt by God's Spirit. No born-again heart, no matter how spiritually alive, if not sanctified to the will of God by the indwelling fullness of the Holy Spirit, can escape hungering to be filled with the Spirit. One may not consciously recognize what the hungering is for, but the nearer the person lives to God, the more he or she will hunger to be filled with the Spirit. What a high and holy calling it is to be filled by God the Holy Spirit. Is this your experience today?

Indwell My Personality

Did You create this soul of mine
    That in me You might fully dwell?
How can You choose a heart like mine?
    My sin made me a child of hell!
O God, if You now want my heart,
    If You choose my heart for Your throne,
Then take possession of each part
    And make me Yours and Yours alone!

Indwell my being through and through;
    Your Spirit in my spirit live.
My inmost self I give to You—
    My will, my mind, my love I give.
Live out Your nature now in mine
    In all its lovely holiness.
Your Spirit's fruit let others see
    As You through me show love and bless.

See through my eyes, think through my mind;
    Your nature within mine display.
Will through my will till others find
    My self is crucified alway.
No longer 'twill be I who live—
    Not I but You, Lord, live in me.
Your holy disposition give—
    Your presence, pow'r, and purity.

O Christian friends, I dare not boast;
    I'm less than nothing in myself.

What you see is His holiness;
    Anything good is of His wealth.
He gives His vict'ry over sin;
    He reigns within me hour by hour.
He lives His holiness within;
    He manifests His gracious pow'r.

My testimony is of God,
    Of all He does each day in me.
He sheds His holy love abroad
    Filling my personality.
No praise to me; all praise to Him
    Who does so fully me indwell.
May nothing e'er His image dim
    But let me e'er His glory tell.

                                        Wesley L. Duewel

CHAPTER 7

The Infilling of the Holy Spirit

To be filled with God's Spirit, all born-again children of God must experience a definite moment of self-surrender to Him as a living sacrifice for time and eternity (Rom. 12:1). The Holy Spirit from then on becomes Lord of their life, and they, as ones alive from the dead, must deliberately yield to God (6:13), submitting their total personality to holiness (v. 19) through the indwelling of the Holy Spirit. Then the benefits they reap will lead to holiness (v. 22). They will have the fruit of the Spirit in a new fullness as the Spirit floods their whole personality, their innermost being (John 7:38–39). Although this fruit will begin at the new birth, believers will experience carnal hindrances to full development and manifestation until their heart is cleansed from these by the Holy Spirit.

In the moment of new birth, repentant hearts are regenerated by the Spirit of God and persons are adopted into God's family (Eph. 1:5–6) and saved by grace (2:3–5). They are made into a new creation (2 Cor. 5:17), caused to pass from death to life (John 5:24), and are forgiven of all sins (Col. 2:13). The Spirit witnesses that they are now children of God (Rom. 8:16). Many have wondered why at that same instant God does not also cleanse from all inner defilement, put to death the carnal nature, and fill with the Holy Spirit. The New Testament record and the testimony of Christian biography both indicate that this is not how God works.

Many children of God know they have experienced the new birth, know the Spirit witnesses with their spirit that they are

God's children (Rom. 8:16), and yet also know and deplore that there is a carnal nature within that needs cleansing by the blood of Christ (1 John 1:7). There is a self that needs a deeper surrender to God's will, an inner defeat for which Christ has a fuller victory, an inner struggle for which Christ has a perfect rest (Heb. 4:1, 9–11), and a fullness of the Spirit's lordship and ministry they have not yet experienced. They feel the Spirit calling them to a special moment, a crisis of surrender, victory, cleansing, infilling, and empowering.

May This Be the Crisis Hour

How can our Savior tolerate
   Uncleanness in His bride?
How can His holiness, so great,
   In carnal lives take pride?
O Savior, make us fully clean,
No spot of sin in us be seen!

How can our Savior draw us near
   If we are carnal still?
How can we share His fullness here
   Unless we seek His will?
O Savior, give Your purity;
'Tis Your will that we holy be.

How can our hearts be Spirit-filled
   If sinful self remain?
A full salvation You have willed—
   Fulfill in us Your reign.
You are a perfect Conqueror—
Oh, triumph in our spirits now!

We have full faith in all Your Word;
   Your promise we believe.
Your call to holiness we've heard;
   Your grace we now receive.
Oh, may this be the crisis hour
When You descend in holy pow'r.

Wesley L. Duewel

New Testament believers had the same experience of the Holy Spirit. The apostles were truly born of God. Their names were written in heaven (Luke 10:20). They received Christ's Word (John 17:8) and obeyed it (v. 6). Jesus testified five times that they were given to Him by the Father (John 17:2, 6, 9, 24). He said to the Father, "They are yours" (v. 9), and "Glory has come to me through them" (v. 10). Twice He said, "They are not of the world any more than I am of the world" (v. 14, cf. v. 16). It was for them that Christ prayed, "Sanctify them" (v. 17). He breathed the Spirit on them when He restored them from their backsliding (20:22). But it was not until Pentecost that they were filled with the Holy Spirit (Acts 2:4).

The same was true in Samaria. People accepted God's Word (Acts 8:14), believed (v. 12), and were baptized (v. 12). As soon as the apostles heard this, they wanted the new believers to be Spirit-filled (which should be the norm of all New Testament Christian experience)! So they sent Peter and John to pray for them that they might be filled with the Spirit (vv. 15, 17).

The Romans at the home of Cornelius had the same experience. Cornelius was a devout (Acts 10:2), righteous (v. 22), God-fearing man (vv. 2, 22) who prayed (v. 2) and whose prayer was heard (v. 31). He was obviously accepted by God (v. 35). But as Peter preached, these new believers were instantly filled with the Spirit just as the apostles had been (11:15). Peter said, "God, who knows the heart, showed that he accepted them by giving the Holy Spirit to them." He gave the same experience of heart purity (15:8–9) by faith that the apostles had received by faith at Pentecost when they were Spirit-filled.

The Greeks at Ephesus also experienced the same work of the Spirit. These disciples (Acts 19:1) had not yet been filled with the Spirit, and Paul did not want any group of converts to miss out on being Spirit-filled. Paul himself had been converted on the Damascus road, had been addressed by Ananias as a brother-believer (9:17), and then had been filled with the Spirit three days after he met Christ and believed. Further, Christ had clearly demonstrated in His high-priestly prayer in John 17 that the sanctification for which He prayed (v. 17) and for which He died outside the gate (Heb. 13:12) was for believers, not for the unsaved (John 17:9).

God in His sovereign wisdom chose that people should first be forgiven of their sins (plural) before they are cleansed of their sinful nature (sin in the singular). God knew that in repentance people are so convicted over the guilt of their sins that they are largely unaware that they have a defiling sinful nature. God, therefore, chose that the twofold nature of sin should be met by a twofold work of the Spirit.

The cry of the sinner in both the Old and the New Testaments is "I have sinned!" (cf. Ps. 51:4). The cry of the forgiven child of God convicted of his sinful nature is "I am unclean" (cf. Isa. 6:5). The cry of the first is "I have done," and of the second is "I am." The plea of the first is "Forgive me, pardon me!" The cry of the second is "Sanctify me, cleanse me, fill me!"

For the first there is the washing away of sins by Christ's blood (Rev. 1:5). Our committed acts of sin—whether by thought, word, or deed—are always referred to in the plural. Our unholy nature is referred to always in the singular. For it there is cleansing by the blood also (1 John 1:7). The cleansing of sin is typified by the baptism of Holy Spirit fire. It is also pictured as crucifixion of our carnal-self life.

Give Me a Crucified Heart

Give me a heart that is crucified;
Give me a heart that with You has died.
    Give me a life that is one with God,
    Cleansed by the flow of Your precious blood.

Give me a heart that is dead to self.
Dead to this world, to its pomp and wealth,
    Dead to its pride, to its search for fame,
    Dead to attempts to exalt its name.

Nail my old nature upon Your cross
Until earth's gain I can count but loss,
    Till unto me all the world has died
    As I unto it am crucified.

Give me a crucified, humble mind,
Tender, compassionate, meek, and kind.
    Give me a crucified, yielded will
    Ready at once any call to fill.

May my affections be crucified,
Perfect in love, though most sorely tried,
    Make all my being, yes all of me
    Nailed to Your cross upon Calvary.

Lord, may Your death e'er in me prevail;
Free not my self from the driven nail.
   Keep me each moment, Lord, crucified,
   Nailed to Your cross by Your riven side.

Wesley L. Duewel

It is true that persons once filled with the Spirit may be filled again and again with the Spirit to new overflowing as they keep walking in the light and surrender to the Spirit's lordship. For every new need or crisis or call, God can give new anointing, new empowering, new infilling, as seen in the book of Acts. But the Spirit-filled life must always be entered into initially at a moment when we first are filled. This is always based on our act of full surrender. God does not call sinners to offer themselves as a sacrifice. He wants them to repent. Sinners have nothing to offer to God but their sins. But born-again believers are alive to God, and they can present themselves as living sacrifices and yield themselves in an act of consecration (Rom. 6:11–13, 18–19). The prerequisite to faith for the forgiveness of sins is repentance; the prerequisite to faith for the infilling of the Spirit is entire consecration (1 Thess. 5:23–24). This entire sanctification or complete filling with the Spirit is for those who are already members of Christ's body, the church (Eph. 5:25–27; 1 Thess. 5:23).

Sanctification, or being full of the Spirit, does not make it impossible to sin, but it does enable believers to be in constant victory over sin. It does not save from temptation, but it does give power to be victorious over temptation. The Holy Spirit gives us power to be what God calls us to be (1 Peter 1:15–16), to be holy as He is holy. The sanctified life is not a life of sinless perfection in which it is impossible to sin and impossible to grow. On the contrary, it is life in which it is possible to be victor over sin and in which it becomes gloriously possible to begin the greatest life of growth in grace, of progressive maturity, of progressive sanctification. The crisis of cleansing and initial infilling of the Spirit begin a life of constant cleansing and infilling as long as we walk in the light (1 John 1:7).

The tragedy is that so many born-again children of God go on living in spiritual defeat without the crisis of full surrender and cleansing, without the infilling and empowering God promises (Acts 2:39) to all who obey (5:32), have faith (15:9), and ask

(Luke 11:13). What is this fullness of the Holy Spirit, or full sanctification? It is that crisis of appropriation, that instantaneous experience by faith, subsequent to the new birth, wherein the blood of Christ's atonement cleanses from all sin and the Holy Spirit fills and empowers for holy living the believer who is wholly devoted to the love and service of God.

No one sign or gift of the Spirit is the necessary evidence of this precious experience, for the Holy Spirit is His own witness in the soul (Heb. 10:15). The essential fact at Pentecost was not the outward symbols of wind, fire, or tongues, but the purifying of believers' hearts by faith (Acts 15:9). The proof of this fullness of the Spirit in His total lordship is His abiding presence performing His holy work—continuously applying Christ's blood (1 John 1:7), empowering us for victorious and radiant living (2 Cor. 3:17–18), and anointing us for prayer (Rom. 8:25–27; Jude 20) and witness (Acts 1:8). He makes each Spirit-filled believer God's gift to the church to build up the church and make it effective in completing Christ's redemptive ministry (1 Cor. 12:18). The Holy Spirit supplies as He chooses whatever enabling, endowment, enduement, or gift is required by a believer to fulfill his or her God-appointed role (v. 11).

Sanctification is begun in the new birth and is made entire the moment one is filled with the Spirit—that is, when the cleansing from all sin becomes complete (1 Thess. 5:23). Sanctification is continued by the Holy Spirit as He leads the Spirit-filled believer to ever-increasing maturity (Phil. 3:12–15), ever-increasing glory (2 Cor. 3:18), and ever-increasing Christlikeness (Eph. 4:13).

Make Me Pure Like You

Did You, my Savior, for me die
To cleanse and fill and sanctify?
   Did You, Lord, suffer on the cross
   To purify from sin and dross?
Then shed on me Your searching light
Till I am pure in heaven's sight.

I would receive Your cleansing new;
I would be pure even as You.
   Sanctification is Your will;
   Lord, all Your will in me fulfill.

This promise, Lord, You did inspire—
Oh send to me Your cleansing fire.

I seek all You have promised me—
Your promise, Lord, is purity.
  Since You did holiness command,
  On my soul place Your purging hand.
O You Who baptize us with fire,
Baptize me just as You desire.

Let me be in Your spotless bride
Pure as we stand there by Your side,
  So pure that You can joyfully
  Include me in Your company.
Unworthy of You though I be,
I'll ever sing Your love to me.

So, Lord, perfect Your will in me
Till You delight my life to see.
  You, Lord, have asked my perfect love;
  You must bestow it from above,
Till I am all that You design
As You forevermore are mine.

Wesley L. Duewel

CHAPTER 8

The Special Moment of Infilling

Some people who are truly born again may not remember the exact moment when they confessed their sins and trusted Christ for forgiveness. They may not have used the word *repentance,* but in their heart they did repent of their sins and trust Jesus to forgive them. They did receive Christ as their Savior— that is, they were born again, even if they did not know or use the theological term *born again* as Jesus used it in John 3:3, 7.

Similarly, some people have taken steps to be filled with the Spirit without fully realizing what they were doing. I knew a saintly grandmother who had never heard clear theological preaching. When she heard a message on being filled with the Spirit, she began to praise the Lord. "That has been my experience for forty years," she joyfully testified; "I just didn't know what to call it."

Some people have been prejudiced against being filled with the Spirit by other people's comments but nevertheless have been led by the Holy Spirit into His fullness. They have a holy heart undisturbed by sinful character traits, such as envy, jealousy, carnal anger, impurity, greed, and hatred. Because of their prejudice, they may not realize that they are truly Spirit-filled. God understands, for He knows their hearts and fills them with the Holy Spirit. Being filled with the Spirit is not a denominational matter; it is a heart experience.

Normally, however, there is a special moment when the soul is ready and hungry to be filled, having met all of God's conditions, when faith grasps God's promise and makes it one's own. It is a special, definitive moment of spiritual victory when the Spirit takes complete lordship of a Christian's life and the Christian submits to God's sovereignty. In the new birth, a sinner gives up rebellion but may still harbor some things in the heart that react against God's sovereignty. When a Christian unreservedly consecrates himself or herself to God, He in the fullest sense is welcomed as Sovereign and Lord.

An illustration from American history can help us understand this. At the close of the Civil War, General Robert E. Lee, commander-in-chief of the southern armed forces, surrendered to General Ulysses Grant, commander-in-chief of the rest of the United States. The two generals met by appointment for the official act of surrender. At long last there was to be peace—the nation would be reunited.

They met at the appointed place. General Lee, in his full military uniform as general of the armies of the South, advanced toward General Grant and extended his hand to shake Grant's hand. Grant stood, unmoving. He said simply, "First your sword." Lee understood. He removed his sword and handed it to Grant handle first. Symbolically he was saying, "The fight is over. I surrender my arms to you." Grant took the sword and handed it to his assistant. He then extended his right hand to Lee. The war was over.

The moment General Lee surrendered he became an ordinary citizen. In total surrender he gave up his sword with all it symbolized. Spiritually, that is what takes place when sinners repent. Until that moment they are spiritually in rebellion against God, but then they give up their sword. Thus, they receive forgiveness and enter Christ's kingdom.

Once General Lee was no longer a rebel, he was again an accepted and honored citizen who offered his cooperation. Similarly, when sinners repent and are forgiven, they are instantly accepted as children of God who can give themselves to God in obedience and service. On the other hand, unrepentant sinners have nothing to give to God. Since the Bible clearly says, "If anyone does not have the Spirit of Christ, he does not belong to Christ" (Rom. 8:9), the Spirit-filled life is only for Christians, who in deep consecration and commitment, give themselves totally to God in gratitude.

In the moment when you as a born-again Christian are filled with the Spirit, four things take place in your life:

1. *The Holy Spirit instantly becomes Lord in your life.* Have you yielded yourself in total surrender, given yourself as an offering to God? If you have, you can now say with Paul: "I have been crucified with Christ and I no longer live, but Christ lives in me. The life I live in the body, I live by faith in the Son of God, who loved me and gave himself for me" (Gal. 2:20); and "We know that our old self was crucified with him so that the body of sin might be done away with, that we should no longer be slaves to sin—because anyone who has died has been freed from sin" (Rom. 6:6–7).

As a Christian you are now able to fulfill Romans 12:1. Note that this verse is addressed to "brothers"—that is, to Christians. No unforgiven sinner can fulfill this verse: "Therefore, I urge you, brothers, in view of God's mercy, to offer your bodies as living sacrifices, holy and pleasing to God—this is your spiritual act of worship" (Rom. 12:1). In a moment of absolute surrender, you yield yourself spirit, soul, and body—all of your being—to the Lord. This act of total surrender is pleasing to God and opens you to the fullness of the Spirit.

2. *You are instantly cleansed from all sin in the moment of your total surrender.* Notice that this is "sin" in the singular (1 John 1:7). Your many "sins" (plural) were forgiven in the new birth, but your sinful nature, indicated by sin in the singular, is now cleansed by the blood of Christ applied by the Holy Spirit. To use another Bible picture, you are circumcised, and the sinful nature is put off (Col. 2:11). You are forgiven and cleansed from the defilement of committed sins in the new birth. But the sinful nature you inherited from Adam when you were born is not cleansed until as a born-again Christian you totally consecrate your being to God and He takes complete control and fills you.

3. *The Holy Spirit instantly gives you His power.* Jesus promised His disciples that when the Spirit came upon them (at Pentecost), they would receive power (Acts 1:8). From then on there are repeated references in the New Testament to the Spirit's power in believers' lives. The Holy Spirit fills children of God with His holy presence, purity, and power—primarily, power to be holy as God wills for us to be; and secondarily, power for witness and service. He doesn't give His power primarily so that we can do spectacular things, but so that we can live beautiful, holy lives and manifest the fruit of the Spirit (Gal. 5:22–23). God can, however, give miracle-working power to those He chooses.

4. *Spiritual growth can now begin in Spirit-blessed fullness.*
Spiritual growth begins the moment a person becomes a child of
God. But when carnal hindrances are cleansed away after a person
is filled with the Spirit, the process of spiritual growth is
intensified and accelerated. Just as a garden grows more
luxuriantly when the weeds are removed, so the fruit of the Spirit
grow more gloriously when the weeds of jealousy, envy, pride,
self-will, and stubbornness are cleansed away by the fullness of
the Spirit.

The holy process of transfiguration, spiritual growth that is
aided, guided, and enabled by the Holy Spirit, can become blessedly
real. When a person is Spirit-filled, acts of obedience, self-
discipline, and prayer cause the process of transfiguration to surge
forward in waves of personal spiritual progress unto Christlikeness.

CHAPTER 9

Spirit-Filled Examples

Spirit-filled lives are beautiful examples of God's presence, Christ's beauty, and the Spirit's working. Being Spirit-filled has nothing to do with one's denomination, and Spirit-filled people do not necessarily all state their doctrine of the Holy Spirit in the same terms. They are born-again Christians who made a total surrender of themselves to Jesus, asking that the Holy Spirit completely fill, cleanse, and empower them. As a result, they are spiritually victorious and filled with love for God, His Word, His family, and the whole world.

In this chapter I give a few examples of Christians who were well-known for living a Spirit-filled life. May their examples make us hungry to draw closer to God and live a Spirit-filled life. Over the centuries millions of God's children have been filled. So can you if you meet God's simple conditions.

We may be a humble, little-known Christian and still be Spirit-filled. We are not Spirit-filled nor can we become Spirit-filled if we secretly want to impress others with our spirituality. We are Spirit-filled to be wholly God's, to be truly Christlike, and to be available to God for anything He wills for us.

It is a joy to present as examples John Bunyan, author of *Pilgrim's Progress* and prisoner for Jesus; Charles G. Finney, one of God's greatest soul winners whom God used in revival; Dwight L. Moody, untrained, uneducated evangelist whom God used to bless America; and Oswald Chambers, Bible teacher and YMCA worker during World War I.

You can be just as Spirit-filled as they. You need not be famous, highly educated, or financially prosperous. All you need is a fully surrendered, spiritually hungry heart that loves to commune with God in prayer and seeks to obey God in everything.

John Bunyan

John Bunyan, author of *Pilgrim's Progress,* grew up godless and constantly blaspheming God. He was a terror to others. One day he overheard three or four women talking about a work of God in their souls, which they called "new birth." God had changed their souls with His love. Bunyan did not understand what they were talking about but was deeply affected. He tried to reform himself, and after he was married and his wife had taught him to read, he began reading the Bible. At times the Bible encouraged him, and at other times some verses seemed to leave him hopeless.

One day God used John 6:37, "Him that cometh to me, I will in no wise cast out" (KJV), to set him spiritually free. When Satan would accuse him, Bunyan clung to this promise. He said, "God be praised, I overcame [Satan]; I got sweetness from it."[1]

Later God taught Bunyan about union with Christ, and he was evidently filled with the Spirit. He saw that Jesus Christ was "made unto us wisdom, and righteousness, and sanctification, and redemption" (1 Cor. 1:30 KJV). "I never saw such heights and depths of grace, and love, and mercy." He told that several times the grace of God was so real to him that "I could hardly bear up under it, and it was so out of measure amazing. . . . I do think if that sense of it had abode long upon me it would have made me incapable for business. . . . The glory of the holiness of God did at this time break me to pieces."[2]

Bunyan tells about one night when Christ was especially near to him. "Christ was a precious Christ to my soul that night; I could scarce lie in bed for joy, and peace, and triumph through Christ. . . . "I saw myself within the arms of grace and mercy; and though I was before afraid to think of a dying hour, yet, now I cried, 'Let me die'; now death was lovely and beautiful in my sight."

While in prison, this Spirit-filled man of God wrote, "I never had in all my life so great an inlet into the Word of God as now. . . . Jesus Christ also was never more real and apparent than now." *Pilgrim's Progress* was his vision-dream describing the Christian life. In it he saw "two shining ones" who had loved the Lord Jesus when in the world, and as they entered heaven's gate, "they were transfigured; and they had raiment put on that shone like gold, and a voice rang out, 'enter ye into the joy of your Lord.'"[3] What glory to crown Spirit-filled lives!

Charles G. Finney

Charles G. Finney, a twenty-nine-year-old lawyer, was for several days deeply convicted by the Holy Spirit of his personal sinfulness. He determined to seek God's forgiveness, and on the morning of October 10, 1821, he was born again while praying in the woods near his home. That evening in his office he was wonderfully filled with the Spirit. He testified:

> I received a mighty baptism of the Holy Ghost without any expectation of it, without ever having the thought in my mind that there was any such thing for me, without any recollection that I had ever heard the thing mentioned by any person in the world, the Holy Spirit descended upon me in a manner that seemed to go through me body and soul. I could feel the impression, like a wave of electricity, going through and through me. Indeed, it seemed to come in waves and waves of liquid love....
>
> No words can express the wonderful love that was shed abroad in my heart. I wept aloud with joy and love.... These waves came over me and over me and over me, one after another, until I recollect I cried out, "I shall die if these waves continue to pass over me." I said, "Lord, I cannot bear any more." Yet I had no fear of death....
>
> When I awoke in the morning ... instantly the baptism that I had received the night before returned upon me in the same manner.... The Spirit seemed to say to me, "Will you doubt? Will you doubt?" I cried, "No! I will not doubt; I cannot doubt." He then cleared the subject up so much to my mind that it was in fact impossible for me to doubt that the Spirit of God had taken possession of my soul.[4]

Dr. V. Raymond Edman summarizes Finney's experience: "By the Spirit of God, Finney came under deep conviction, learned God's plan of salvation, and was born again of the Spirit; then without his knowledge of any such experience was filled to over-flowing with the Spirit!"[5]

It is most unusual for the fullness of the Spirit to come with such overwhelming emotion. It may be a very quiet experience, and usually it comes after a deliberate full surrender of one's spirit, life, and all to God as one's soul cries out to God to be filled.

Dwight L. Moody

Dwight L. Moody, one of the world's greatest evangelists, had a thrilling testimony. When he was converted at age seventeen on April 21, 1855, he lived in great poverty, and he could scarcely read or write. He had had a total of about five years of schooling.

When Moody was eighteen, he moved to Chicago and almost immediately asked permission to teach a Sunday school class. He recruited his own class from poor children from Chicago slums. He soon had so many children that the church could not hold them. He then started a separate Sunday school, and in a few years his Sunday school grew to fifteen hundred people.

Moody had a tremendous passion for souls. He began ministering to the parents of the children and speaking each day and night to men in a nearby army camp. He was soon speaking three times a day. His Sunday school became a church, and hundreds were saved. His church became the largest in Chicago.

Two of Moody's faithful female members sat on the front seat in every service with their heads down, praying. They told him at the close of each service that they were praying for him to receive God's power. Moody told them to pray for the people. Yes, they affirmed, they were doing that, but they were also praying for God's power to become his. He thought he had God's power, but the Holy Spirit began to convict him of his need for the fullness of the Spirit, and he had them pray with him. By 1871 he was truly hungering and thirsting to be filled with the Spirit. His church and all around it had been burned down in the great Chicago fire of 1871.

One day Moody was walking up Wall Street in New York City and his heart was crying out to God for the Spirit's fullness. God's power came upon him so strongly that he had to hurry to the house of a friend and ask if he might have a room by himself. He stayed in that room alone for hours, and the Holy Spirit came upon him, filling his soul with such joy and such an overwhelming sense of God's presence that he had to ask God "to withhold His hand, lest he die on the spot from very joy. He went out from that place with the power of the Holy Spirit upon him."[6]

Torrey writes, "Time and again Mr. Moody would come to me and say: 'Torrey, I want you to preach on the baptism with the Holy Ghost [the term he used for the fullness of the Spirit].' I do not know how many times he asked me to speak on that subject."

Whenever Moody had a campaign or series of meetings, he would ask Torrey to preach two messages, one entitled "Ten Reasons Why I Believe the Bible to be the Word of God" and the other entitled "The Baptism with the Holy Ghost." Torrey adds, "Time and again, when a call came to me to go off to some church, he would come up to me and say: 'Now, Torrey, be sure and preach on the baptism with the Holy Ghost.'"[7]

Torrey concludes his booklet:

I shall never forget the eighth of July, 1894, to my dying day. It was the closing day at the Northfield Students' Conference—the gathering of the students from the eastern colleges. Mr. Moody had asked me to preach on Saturday night and Sunday morning on the baptism with the Holy Ghost. On Saturday night I had spoken about, "The Baptism with the Holy Ghost: What It Is; What It Does; The Need of It and the Possibility of It." On Sunday morning I spoke on "The Baptism with the Holy Spirit: How to Get It."

It was just exactly twelve o'clock when I finished my morning sermon, and I took out my watch and said, "Mr. Moody has invited us all to go up on the mountain at three o'clock this afternoon to pray for the power of the Holy Spirit. It is three hours to three o'clock. Some of you cannot wait three hours. You do not need to wait. Go to your rooms; go out into the woods; go to your tent; go anywhere you can get alone with God and have this matter out with Him." At three o'clock we all gathered in front of Mr. Moody's mother's house (she was then still living), and then began to pass down the lane, through the gate, up on the mountainside. There were 456 of us in all; I know the number because Paul Moody counted us as we passed through the gate.

After a while Mr. Moody said, "I don't think we need to go any further; let us sit down here." We sat down on stumps and logs and on the ground. Mr. Moody said, "Have any of you students anything to say?" I think about seventy-five of them arose, one after another, and said, "Mr. Moody, I could not wait till three o'clock; I have been alone with God since the morning service, and I believe I have a right to say that I have been baptized with the Holy Spirit." When these testimonies were over, Mr. Moody said, "Young men, I can't see any reason why we shouldn't kneel down here right now and ask God that the Holy Spirit may fall upon us just as definitely as He fell upon the apostles on the Day of Pentecost. Let us pray." And we did pray, there on the mountainside. . . . The Holy Ghost fell upon us. Men and women, that is what we all need— the baptism with the Holy Ghost.[8]

Oswald Chambers

The writings of Oswald Chambers, primarily his daily devotional book *My Utmost for His Highest,* have been a blessing throughout this century. He was a friend of Charles Cowman, founder of OMS International, a missionary society in which I have worked for some sixty years. He, too, lived a Spirit-filled life.

Chambers was born in Scotland in 1874, the son of a Baptist pastor. He was converted on hearing Charles H. Spurgeon preach; met William Quarrier, who founded orphan homes in Scotland; and learned from him the principles of faith and prayer. After his conversion he felt led to withdraw from Edinburgh University, and he entered a little-known Baptist college at Dunoon to prepare for the ministry.

Chambers knew he was a born-again child of God, but he felt it was absolutely necessary for the fire to come upon his soul. He became a tutor in the college, still longing for the fullness of the Spirit. After hearing a message by Dr. F. B. Meyer (who emphasized "the deeper life") at the college, Chambers "determined to have all God had for him," and for four years he prayed incessantly for "the baptism of the Holy Ghost"—that is, the cleansing fullness of the Spirit. He was very oppressed by his sense of inner depravity. God used him for the conversion of others, but the Bible seemed dull and most uninteresting. He sensed over and over his own sinful carnality and the vileness in his soul. He referred to it as "the plague" of his heart. The Holy Spirit taught him and used circumstances to show him how sinful his own heart was. He described that period as "four years of hell on earth," though he preached as usual and people were saved and blessed. In his own soul, however, there was darkness and misery.

A series of meetings was held in Dunoon for the deepening of the spiritual life of the people. Chambers had heard people talk about the fullness of the Spirit, but he didn't know anyone who claimed to be filled with the Spirit. God spoke to his heart through Luke 11:13, "If ye then, being evil, know how to give good gifts unto your children: how much more shall *your* heavenly Father give the Holy Spirit to them that ask him?" (KJV). He felt so sinful. How could he ask God to give him the Holy Spirit? But then he realized that his receiving the fullness of the Spirit would be a gift from God. After the close of the service one night, a special meeting for prayer was held. Chambers rose to his feet and said, "Either Christianity is a downright fraud, or I have not got hold of the right end of the stick." Right there as he stood, he claimed the gift of the Holy Spirit, trusting the promise of Luke 11:13. He had no special emotional blessing. He only knew that he had taken God at His word.

A few days later Chambers was asked to speak at a meeting, and there forty people came forward to seek salvation. Terrified, he went to the principal of the Bible college: "What shall I do?" The principal said, "Don't you remember you asked God to give you the gift of His Spirit, and you claimed it by faith? Didn't Jesus say, 'Ye shall receive power'? This is God's power from on high."

Chambers said of his experience:

> If the previous years had been hell on earth, these next four years have truly been heaven on earth. Glory be to God, the last aching abyss of the human heart is filled to overflowing with the love of God. Love is the beginning, love is the middle, and love is the end. After He comes in, all you see is "Jesus only, Jesus ever." When you know what God has done for you, the power and the tyranny of sin is gone and the radiant, unspeakable emancipation of the indwelling Christ has come, and when you see men and women who should be princes and princesses with God bound up in a show of things—oh, you begin to understand what the

apostle meant when he said he wished that he himself were accursed from Christ that men might be saved.[9]

The remaining years of Chambers' life are a testimony to the reality of the fullness of the Spirit he received that night. He said, "Abandonment of ourselves is the kernel of consecration, not presenting our gifts, but presenting ourselves without reserve. We too through the crisis of a complete surrender, may receive a divine anointing (1 John 2:20), preparing us for effective service. We however, unlike our sinless Lord, need not only the holy anointing but also the cleansing fire (Acts 2:3)." Oswald Chambers always insisted on the need for a "mighty baptism of the Holy Spirit" as the birthright of every believer. He taught that "sanctification is the very holiness of Jesus, His peace, His joy, His purity, imparted to us by the Holy Spirit, and received by faith."[10]

J. E. Fison, Anglican bishop of Salisbury, wrote in his tribute to Oswald Chambers: "It is impressive to see in Oswald Chambers a man who experienced a most definite 'second blessing' of sanctification, and yet pass on, not to deny the crucial importance of Luke 11:13—a text which he always kept on using in personal work—but to an even greater faith in and reliance on the inexhaustible riches of the person of our Lord regardless of all 'varieties of religious experience' or lack of them."

Oswald Chambers lived in his Bible, reading and studying it constantly. He was also a man of ceaseless prayer. Speaking about his spiritual life and the fullness of the Spirit, he said, "It is no wonder that I talk so much about an altered disposition: God altered mine; I was there when He did it, and I have been there ever since."[11] One who knew Chambers wrote, "To hear him pray was to be in the presence of God; like Murray M'Cheyne and Samuel Rutherford, he seemed to live in uninterrupted communion with God."[12]

Another described Chambers' ministry: "Truly the persuasive power and influence of the Holy Spirit rested upon his works.... There was no excitement, the meetings were quiet and the mighty power of the Holy Spirit was manifested in every service."[13] Wrote another: "I shall never forget the atmosphere of the first meeting, a devotional one, as one entered the room it was like stepping into heaven. Then Mr. Chambers spoke, leading us straight to God, and I afterwards found that this was characteristic of him, in every lecture or meeting he brought one right into the presence of God."[14]

During Chambers' last several years, he ministered to British troops as a YMCA worker in an army training camp in Egypt. One who was there said:

> The salient thing in my memory of that Mission is the way in which there emerged all the time and every time, [Chambers'] own personal, passionate devotion to Jesus Christ. That, and the strange way in which his own self was absent; indeed, that was one of the strangest things about his personality, he inwardly was so intensely there and yet so absolutely absent. There was no self to consider. I recollect well how for long enough I really doubted the possibility of such a thing in him, or in any man or woman, until, watching his life, I became convinced.[15]

Another person reported of Chambers' during his ministry to the troops, "Morning by morning he waited upon God. It was there that he gained the radiance that shone from his face and the message sharper than any two-edged sword."[16] Wherever he went the atmosphere seemed to be charged with the presence of God as he constantly prayed that it might be.

Not everyone can be an Oswald Chambers, but everyone can be filled with the Spirit. We all have our individual roles to play, but we can all glorify God by a Spirit-filled life wherever we are, showing the beauty of a holy heart and anointed living. No two testimonies are identical, but over and over in fulfillment of Acts 2:39, God has fulfilled His promise. All who are filled receive the Spirit's gracious cleansing and inner empowering for holy living and for whatever service God may choose for them. Do not hunger for God to repeat the identical emotional details that you read about, but ask Him to repeat the reality and the inner spirituality of the fullness of the Spirit in you. God does not show favoritism. In keeping with His promises and His plan for your life, when He fills you with His Spirit, He will give you inner transforming Christlikeness and new spiritual power.

CHAPTER 10

Faith: The Appropriating Means of the Fullness of the Spirit

Paul was sent by God for a twofold ministry: that the nations might receive (1) the forgiveness of sins and (2) sanctification by faith (Acts 26:18). The fullness of the Spirit is given to those who ask in faith (Luke 11:13; Acts 15:8–9). It is received by faith just as the new birth is received by faith. It was not just for the apostles or for the early church; rather, "the promise is for you and your children and for all who are far off—for all whom the Lord our God will call" (Acts 2:39). To what promise does this verse refer? To the promise of the Father (Luke 24:49) that by the ministry of the Holy Spirit, Christ's followers will be endued with power from on high. Christ had commanded His own to wait for the fulfillment of this glorious promise (Acts 1:4) that would bring the Holy Spirit's power (v. 8), and it was fulfilled at Pentecost.

We obtain the power of the Holy Spirit by faith for our Christian life on earth. We are to be holy as God is holy (1 Peter 1:15–16). He will sanctify us "through and through" and keep us blameless (1 Thess. 5:23–24) in our earthly life, and we are to serve Him without fear in holiness and righteousness (Luke 1:74–75). Since we are to receive the infilling of the Spirit by faith, it is for all today. We need not wait till death, and we cannot earn it by anything we do ourselves.

It is by obedient faith that we are filled with the Spirit (Acts 5:32), and it is also by faith that we maintain our walk in the Spirit (1 John 1:7). Walking and living in the Spirit empowers us and keeps us pure (Rom. 8:4; Gal. 5:16). Many may have received the infilling of the Spirit by faith but have failed to walk in the life of obedient faith. They confess that they are not Spirit-filled, Spirit-cleansed, Spirit-empowered today. If this is your condition, the same spiritual hunger, the same total surrender in full consecration, the same obedience and simple faith that opened your being to the initial fullness of the Spirit can bring again the fullness of the Spirit. Since the temple of your body was created to be Spirit-filled, you can never be fully satisfied spiritually or be effective as God desires you to be unless you daily live a Spirit-filled life.

Real faith is so simple that it can easily be superficial and become nothing more than mental gymnastics. However, neither saving faith nor sanctifying faith is mere mental assent. Many unsaved persons have mentally assented to truth without being transformed because they failed to meet God's conditions.

We may ask someone, "Do you believe that you are a sinner?"

"Yes."

"Do you believe that Christ died to save sinners?"

"Yes."

"Read this promise. Do you believe that this promise is true?"

"Yes."

"Then, thank God, you are saved!"

But is he? Only if he has met God's conditions. But did he? If he is still unrepentant, no matter how many times he goes over the above formula, he remains unsaved and untransformed.

Saving faith involves consent of the will—obedience—as well as mental assent. Obedience is manifested in repentance. Saving faith begins with assent to the truth, proceeds to consent of the will in true obedience, and finally appropriates by faith. By faith we claim God's forgiveness and make it our own. We can exercise this trust because we know we have met God's condition of repentance. Apart from this full exercise of saving faith, there is no new birth. The demons themselves are forced to assent to the truth. Scripture says that they believe and shudder, but this does nothing to save them (James 2:19).

Some people who have had a merely nominal acceptance of Christ without a clear experience of the new birth may later have truly repented and come into such a glorious experience of the new birth that they thought they were at that moment filled with the Spirit. They may have testified to this for a while until they found sinful tendencies and defeat still in their lives. They have thus ceased to believe full cleansing is possible. "I tried it and it didn't work" is their testimony.

Others may have been born again, but in seeking to be Spirit-filled they have merely gone through some form of mental gymnastics. We may ask someone, "Do you believe that God can sanctify and fill with His Spirit?"

"Yes."

"Read 1 John 1:7. Do you believe that God means what He says in this promise?"

"Yes."

"Well, praise God, you are filled with the Spirit!"

But is she? If she has not met God's conditions of full obedience and full consecration, she has merely given mental assent.

Others have believed some emotional experience to be the filling with the Spirit. On some occasion when they felt God's presence in a special way, they concluded that they were now filled with the Spirit. But if they did not surrender their will to God, they were not filled, for faith without consecration does not bring the fullness of the Spirit. Consecration leading to sanctification and the infilling of the Spirit is a matter of the will, not just of the mind or emotions. The Spirit-filled life has holy emotion, for the Spirit fills with rivers of love, joy, and peace. But emotion is not the proof of nor the measure of the Spirit.

Emotions are related to many factors. If God moves deeply and emotionally, thank Him for it. Tears and joy are precious if they are Spirit-produced. But remember that emotions make you neither more nor less spiritual than others. Some people weep easily and rejoice easily; others feel just as deeply but do not manifest it outwardly. The measure of our Spirit-filled life is not our emotions, but our consistent commitment to an obedient walk of faith. Salvation in all its aspects is by faith and not by feeling.

I sincerely professed to be filled with the Spirit before I actually was. One day, to my surprise, God showed me depths of pride and anger that remained in my heart and kept me from inner victory. I knew, however, that God had made provision for complete victory. When He showed me my need, I began to search my heart before Him to see if there was anything further I could do to obey. I knew that often God could not answer prayer until we asked forgiveness of others or obeyed Him if there were something He had asked of us (Matt. 5:23–24).

But as I searched my heart, I could find no such steps that were in my way. God did show me what an abomination my carnal, uncrucified heart was in His sight, and I confessed the depth of my personal need. But I was not discouraged. If I was still carnal, I knew God had made adequate provision at the cross to cleanse me. I came to the place where I had met every condition, and, claiming God's promise, I stepped out in faith, thanking Him that He was faithful to His Word. For the moment I had absolutely no emotional experience of any kind. But I knew I had met God's conditions and made a full surrender, and I knew I had believed God's promise to cleanse and fill me.

I was a college student at the time. In my first class the next morning, I obtained the permission of the teacher to say a word to the class. I gave a simple testimony, confessing that I had been professing to be Spirit-filled but that God had shown me the inner defeats of pride and anger in my own heart. I had not manifested these outwardly, but in my heart I knew I was defeated. I told the class I had met God's conditions of consecration, obedience, and faith, and now He had sanctified and filled me.

Before that day was over, another defeated person came to me, and I was able to lead him into the life of victory. What floods of assurance and joy now swept over my own soul! It seemed as if the cleansing blood washed me through and through. I was flooded with holy emotion as I obeyed the Lord.

God immediately gave the fruit of the Spirit (Gal. 5:22–24) and fruit in soul-winning in an abundance I had never known before. The Holy Spirit became my Guide in a fullness I had never before experienced. He also energized my prayer life. I was surprised to find that inner resentments, which I had thought were normal in all Christians and which had hitherto been normal in my life, were now gone. I was amazed at the difference and felt so clean in God's sight. The Holy Spirit began to illuminate the Word to my soul. Best of all, He made Jesus much more precious to me than I had ever known.

Your inner defeats are probably different from mine. Your experience of the crisis moment of heart cleansing and the infilling of the Spirit will also be different. No two people have the same personality, the same background, the same need, or the same testimony of steps to victory. But all people can have their personal spiritual needs met at Calvary and can know they are filled with the Spirit, for the Holy Spirit will give His own unmistakable witness in their heart.

We Can't Afford

The Holy Spirit is the One whom we desire the most.
We must have all His life and pow'r that came at Pentecost.
  The needs of men are far too great for us to meet alone;
  Lord, send the Holy Spirit now to make Your presence
    known.

We can't afford to be so weak when He has perfect
    pow'r;
We dare not fail the needs of men who look to us this hour.
  We long to live each moment under His complete control;
  We want His power and His sway o'er body and o'er soul.

We can't afford to miss His plan when He would be our
    Guide;
We can't afford to live one day except as He abide.
  We can't afford to fail Him or to miss His holy will;
  Lord, let the Spirit in us all Your holy plan fulfill.

We can't afford to disappoint or fail to meet Your test;
We can't afford to carry on with only second best.
  This is the only life we have. We give it totally;
  Lord, send the Spirit now to us in all His ministry.

Wesley L. Duewel

CHAPTER 11

Steps to the Fullness of the Spirit

What are the steps to being cleansed by, filled with, and empowered by the Spirit? The basis of all is the new birth. You cannot be cleansed from your sinful nature until you have repented and received God's forgiveness of the sins you have committed. When you are saved by God's grace and know that there is nothing between God and you that has broken His fellowship, there are four simple steps to the fullness of the Spirit.

1. Open Your Heart to the Revelation of the Spirit

Just as the Holy Spirit convicts unregenerate sinners of their need of salvation, so the Holy Spirit convicts believers of their need of sanctification and the infilling of the Spirit. The steps of His revelation may occur in a matter of moments or may extend over a period of time. No two testimonies are exactly the same, but sooner or later the Holy Spirit must reveal to you (1) God's will, (2) your soul's need, and (3) God's promise.

You must be convinced that it is God's will for you to be filled with His Spirit here and now. You must know that God commands you to be holy (Lev. 11:44; 1 Peter 1:16), that He calls you to holiness (1 Thess. 4:7), and that only His indwelling Spirit can make you holy. This revelation may come through reading the Word, watching the life of a Spirit-filled person, or listening to a gospel message or testimony.

You must realize the sinfulness of your heart, how full it is of carnal traits and tendencies, and how weak and defeated your life has been. For you, like Isaiah, this may come through some revelation of God's holiness (Isa. 6). Or, like Peter, you may come to the realization of your need through some tragic failure on your own part (Matt. 26:69–75; Mark 14:66–72; Luke 22:54–62; John 18:15–27). The Holy Spirit speaks to our hearts in many ways. He may use the account of the early church in the Acts of the Apostles to show you how far short your life falls of the standard God set therein.

In my case, I was praying alone when the Holy Spirit shed His holy light on 1 Corinthians 13. I had never realized an unrepentant sinner could have a heart so vile in the sight of God as I then realized my carnal, unsanctified heart was in the light of such holy love. I began to loathe my own heart's condition something like Paul must have done in Romans 7. But my heart did not despair, for not only did the Holy Spirit show me the vileness of my own heart, He also showed me God's promise and met my need.

The Holy Spirit must quicken to your heart God's promise to cleanse and fill you. How wonderful is the way the Holy Spirit can take some promise from God's Word and apply it personally to you. By so doing, He lifts your eyes from yourself to God, and by faith you make His promise your very own and find God true to His Word.

If you really want a vision of God's holiness and of your heart's vileness, be willing to take time alone with God. Humble yourself before Him. It may take you hours alone with God, but you will thank God the rest of your life that He showed you your inner defeat. Search your heart in the light of God's Word, being utterly honest with yourself before God. Examine your actions and your motives. "Examine yourselves to see whether you are in the faith; test yourselves. Do you not realize that Christ Jesus is in you— unless, of course, you fail the test?" (2 Cor. 13:5). Pray the prayer of Psalm 139:23–24: "Search me, O God, and know my heart; test me and know my anxious thoughts. See if there is any offensive way in me, and lead me in the way everlasting."

Have you ever seen your heart in the light of the cross? Have you ever seen how much your sin cost Jesus? Have you ever seen how infinitely holy God is? How could you ever invite the Holy Spirit to indwell a heart so unholy and unloving as yours? Surely He must cleanse you before He can fill you. If you have never really seen yourself from God's viewpoint, ask Him to show you. How you will thank God when He does. Then you will say with Job, "My ears had heard of you but now my eyes have seen you. Therefore I despise myself and repent in dust and ashes" (Job 42:5–6). When you share Isaiah's vision of God's infinite holiness, you will cry with him, "Woe to me! . . . I am ruined!" (Isa. 6:5). Then God will be able to send fire from the altar (v. 6) and purge away your uncleanness.

Must everyone have such a vision of God's holiness and one's own sinfulness? Perhaps not. But you may never really understand the cup Christ drank for you in the garden unless you do have such a vision. You may never understand why Christ called out, "My God, my God, why have you forsaken me?" on the cross unless you realize how vile were your sins and your sinful nature that caused Christ to suffer so (Heb. 13:12). If you would testify to the holiness and love of a heartbroken God, let God break you. If you would make the cross live to others, be crucified with Christ. If you would experience all the glory and triumph of Christ's resurrection power, your sinful nature must die and be buried (Rom. 6:6; Gal. 2:20). If you would share with Paul the triumph of Romans 8, come with him to the utter end of yourself as in Romans 7.

May God deliver us from the superficiality of this age. We need more than polite assent to God's truth, more than cold orthodoxy. We need a broken and contrite heart that has been filled with rivers of the Spirit. Get alone on your knees with God's Word, and give the Holy Spirit time to search your heart. Let Him take as long as He needs. Kneel at the cross until your heart is broken, and let Christ make you whole. You can have new victory and new glory if you are willing to pay the price.

Baptize Me with Your Fire

O You whose eyes of burning flame
    Pierce every human heart,
Beholding every guilt and shame,
    Each unclean, hidden part.
O holy searcher of man's soul,
    By Whom all can be seen,
Search me within, and see the whole
    That I too may be clean.

O You who baptize with Your fire
    Those wholly to You giv'n,
Burn all my chaff and false desire

And make me pure as heav'n.
Refine my nature through and through
    Till all is clean and pure,
Till all remaining to Your view
    Is of Your blessing sure.

Anoint my life with holy oil;
    Fill me with flaming zeal,
Enable me to work and toil
    And Your empow'ring feel.
O Christ Who did Your Spirit send
    According to Your Word,
Still on Your Spirit we depend
    And wait in one accord.

Baptize each waiting heart today;
    Baptize me, Lord, just now.
We will Your holy will obey;
    At Your pierced feet we bow.
We claim Your promise, Lord, anew
    And feel Your fire descend.
From henceforth constantly endue
    And keep world without end.

Wesley L. Duewel

2. Hunger and Thirst for the Fullness of God

Do you know what it is to hunger and thirst after righteousness, after the fullness of the Spirit? If you do, I can guarantee you on the authority of God's Word that you will be filled (Matt. 5:6). We can never become too hungry for God. The depth of our desire measures the wealth of what we can receive from God. Jacob began wrestling with the angel as a proud, self-sufficient, self-willed man. But as he prayed, he got so hungry that he determined not to let go of the angelic wrestler until he was blessed. The angel asked Jacob his name—which revealed his needy nature. Jacob confessed it then held on until he prevailed. Jacob (meaning supplanter, deceiver), after his night of prayer, was renamed Israel (Prince with God). He also received the blessing he so much needed (Gen. 32:8–13, 24–30; Hos. 12:4).

Moses became hungry to see God's glory and kept holding on and pleading until God gave him what he desired. We do not know how much of the forty days were spent hungering and thus communing with God. However long it took, Moses received what he hungered for (Ex. 33:18) and came down the mountain aglow with the glory of God (34:29–35).

Are David's prayers mere words? Have you ever really understood the thirst of his soul? He cried out: "O God . . . my soul thirsts for you, my body longs for you, in a dry and weary land. . . . My soul clings to you" (Ps. 63:1–2, 8). "My soul yearns, even faints; . . . my heart and my flesh cry out for the living God" (84:2). "I wait for the Lord, my soul waits. . . . My soul waits for the Lord more than watchmen wait for the morning, more than watchmen wait for the morning" (130:5–6). When your soul thirsts that deeply to be filled with the Spirit, it will not be long until you are filled to overflowing, until a flood tide of blessing flows out from your innermost being to bless parched and thirsty souls all about you.

My mother was converted in her childhood as she knelt at the altar in a country church when the invitation to receive Christ was given. She was too timid to pray aloud, but her heart cried to God for mercy, and she knew God forgave her sins. She felt God's assurance and peace flooding her heart, and the Spirit witnessed to her that she was a child of God. As she knelt there in silence, thanking God for what He had done in giving her the new birth, for some reason God gave her a vision of a ladder stretching up to heaven with angels ascending and descending on it. She thought that all in the church saw it. Just then the evangelist said to the pastor (both were kneeling near her), "God is here!" Mother thought to herself, "Why certainly God is here. Why even His angels are here! Can't you see them?"

But Mother soon found that she had deep spiritual need remaining in her heart. She had an almost uncontrollable temper. She had many sisters and brothers, and often just after she had scrubbed the kitchen floor clean, one sister would deliberately walk across the floor with dirty shoes. On several occasions Mother got so angry that she chased her sister or struck her with a broom. Then she would feel ashamed of her temper and ask God to forgive her. At times her mother would go upstairs in the farm-house, and Mother could hear her weeping and praying for God to deliver her daughter from this temper. My mother would be so ashamed that she would go and weep alone and promise God she would never, never get angry again. But she would!

As a teenager, Mother would read how mightily God had worked in the church during the days of the apostles. As she read the book of Acts, she longed for God to be present like that again. She went to her minister, who told her that such a close walk with God was only for the church in the days of the apostles. As she longed for her spiritual need to be met, the only verse that seemed to hold hope for her was, "Blessed are the poor in spirit" (Matt. 5:3). Feeling that if anyone had spiritual poverty, she was that one, she went to another minister to see if she could claim that promise for herself. He explained it away, and she was left brokenhearted.

One day as Mother went about her work in a home where she was employed, God seemed to whisper to her, "But you are not filled with the Spirit!" "No, Lord," she responded. "But I will not stop praying till I am!" She meant it literally and prayed throughout that day during her work and intended to pray all night, but before morning she fell asleep. When she woke in the morning, she felt ashamed that she had failed to hold on in prayer. She thought, "How can the Lord ever fill me with His Spirit if I don't want it more than this?" All that day she tried to pray on in the hunger of her heart, and that night she resolved to spend the entire night in prayer, but again she fell asleep.

The third morning she was up before the family, praying from the moment she awoke. As she lit the fire in the wood-burning stove to prepare breakfast for the family, she was singing, "Come into my heart, Lord Jesus. There is room in my heart for Thee." Suddenly it seemed the fire from heaven fell upon her heart and the longings of her soul were satisfied. She started from the house to the barn to milk the cow, and she was so happy she began to skip and run for joy. She had never heard a testimony or sermon on the fullness of the Spirit. She had never read a book or article on the subject. But God spoke to her from His own Word. She hardly knew what she was thirsting for, but God knew, and all alone she was filled with the Spirit. From then on she was delivered from her bad temper.

"Blessed are those who hunger and thirst for righteousness, for they will be filled" (Matt. 5:6). You do not need to be able to explain the theology of the Spirit-filled life. All you need is to hunger. Are there defeats in your heart of which you are ashamed?

Are you longing for a victory you know God has for you? Are you hungrier for the fullness of the Spirit than for your daily food? Right now you can, out of the hunger and thirst of your heart, call to God and trust Him to fill you. Open your heart as you read this poem:

Fill Me More and More

O Spirit of the living God,
    Possess my life and soul.
Come, fill and shed Your love abroad
    And take complete control.
I long for all You have for me;
For all Your fullness is my plea.
Oh, come, possess me utterly;
    Blessed Spirit, come.

Chorus:
More and more is what I need;
More and more is all I plead.
    O blessed Spirit, I humbly implore,
    Fill me and use me more and more.

O Spirit of refining fire,
    Cleanse me from ev'ry sin.
With all my heart I do desire
    Your holy flame within.
Burn all that will not stand Your test—
Whate'er cannot by You be blessed.
Oh, fill me with Your holy best;
    Set my life aflame.

O Spirit of redemptive love,
    Pour out Your love through me.
Come, tender Spirit, gentle Dove,
    Give love from Calvary.
Oceans of love to me impart;
May living streams within me start
And flow in love to every heart!
    Love this world through me.

O blessed Spirit, don't delay
    But come and fill with pow'r.
Have in my heart Your perfect way;
    Begin Your work this hour.

Anoint and fill me more and more;
Oh, come upon me o'er and o'er
And use me more than e'er before!
   Come upon me now!

                              Wesley L. Duewel

3. Yield Your All in Full Surrender and Consecration

When you have had a revelation from the Holy Spirit of the
holiness of God and of your own deep need, when you have felt
such unspeakable hunger and such unquenchable thirst for the
fullness of the Spirit, how can you withhold anything from God?
The heart that is consumed with this passion will gladly give its
life, talents, ambitions, possessions, even loved ones in full
surrender to God. This is full consecration. How could you keep
anything back from Him for Whom you long so unspeakably? All
that you are—your past, present, and future—you long to give to
Him Who loved you and died for you.

Let Me Give Myself

Lord, let me give myself fully to You;
All would I consecrate—all, all anew.
   All that I am and have—I bring You all;
   In full surrender at Your feet I fall.

Nothing would I reserve—Spirit divine;
All now I give to You, all that was mine.
   All of my future life is in Your hands;
   I'll obey anything; give Your commands.

Oh, what a joy to give all, all of me!
All Yours for time and for eternity!
   You are responsible from this glad day;
   Speak clearly Your command—I will obey.

From this day onward, Lord, I'm not my own;
You are my sovereign King; my heart, Your throne.
   Have in my life henceforth Your perfect way.
   I'm Yours and Yours alone. Use me, I pray.

                              Wesley L. Duewel

Obedience is no problem when you are hungry for all that God has for you. You will not be able to wait any longer; He cannot fill you too soon. But He cannot fill you until He has all of you. Empty yourself as far as you can. Take your hands off your own life. Let Christ be Lord of all your life, for holiness is Christ living His life within you.

In consecration you transfer the responsibility for your life to God. He has a right as sovereign Lord to tell you how to spend your money, how to use your time, how to make your life choices. He may guide you in paths you have never considered, but He will choose only what is best. You cannot make a mistake when you let God decide for you. He holds your future in His hands. What a privilege! You have no need to worry or fret, because nothing can touch you outside of His will. All things will work together for His glory and your good (Rom. 8:28).

Think of this: God permits us to turn over our unworthy lives to Him, and He willingly accepts the responsibility of our lives from then on. He promises to live and work through us. How we ought to rush to His arms. How dare we hesitate one moment to cast ourselves for time and eternity on the loving heart of God!

Ask and Receive the Spirit

(Luke 11:9–13)

Ask, and it shall be given;
    Seek, and you're sure to find.
Knock, and the door will open—
    Christ has this way designed.
'Tis of the Spirit spoken;
    Ask God, and then believe.
God's Word cannot be broken;
    Ask and you will receive.

If to your precious children
    'Tis your delight to give,
Much more will God in heaven
    Cause Him in you to live.
You need no other merit
    Than Jesus' precious blood;
Ask for the Holy Spirit;

Ask for this Gift of God.

If to a friend at midnight
    You go in search of bread,
Though you do not find one light,
    Though he has gone to bed,
Though he has finished locking,
    Though he has gone to sleep—
If you will keep on knocking
    You will be sure to reap!

Whatever you are needing—
    Purity, unction, pow'r,
Guidance, or help in pleading—
    You can receive this hour.
Praise God, there is no limit
    To what His pow'r can do;
Just now receive His Spirit—
    He will with might endue.

Wesley L. Duewel

4. Appropriate the Spirit's Fullness by Simple Faith

You have seen the infinite purity and holiness of God. You have seen your own unworthiness—the defeats, failures, and vileness of your carnal heart. Your heart cries out to God for help. You hunger to be cleansed, to be made victorious, to be filled with the Spirit of God. You would gladly give your all in utter consecration to God, and you do. What more can you do but rush into His loving arms and cast yourself upon Him for time and eternity? He is waiting to fill you with the fullness of His Spirit. If a human father longs to give good gifts to his children, how much more does your heavenly Father long to give you His best and greatest gift, His Holy Spirit in all His holy fullness (Luke 11:9–13)?

God the Father gave His only Son that you might have a full and free salvation. Would He hesitate to accept you? Christ the beloved Son of God loved the church so much that He gave Himself to sanctify it (Eph. 5:25–27). He longs for His bride to be holy and spotless. Would He hesitate to sanctify you? The Holy Spirit was given to humans to make effective in them God's full plan of salvation. He hovers near, longing to fill us. So bring your empty, hungry heart. Believe and receive, for this is why Christ came to earth (Eph. 1:4) and why God sent the Holy Spirit. The goal of redemption is that God Himself might indwell us. This is the nearest thing we can have on earth to the communion Adam and Eve had with God in Eden. Is this the final goal? No, thank God, no! This is the initial filling, and much more lies ahead.

Praise God for Cleansing Grace

Praise God from whom all blessings flow
What mighty grace He does bestow!
   He comes within the lives of men
   Fulfilling all His will again.

There is no heart bowed in defeat
That cannot kneel at Jesus' feet
   And by His sanctifying pow'r
   Know fullest vict'ry every hour.

There is no heart so full of self
But God can cleanse and fill Himself.
   His promises He will fulfill
   And with His Holy Spirit fill.

This is today His day of grace;
He smiles on you with loving face.
   He longs to make your spirit whole
   And cleanse and beautify your soul.

Praise God from whom all blessings flow
Praise Him and serve Him here below.
   Open your heart to God above
   And He will flood with perfect love.

Wesley L. Duewel

PART 2

Be Transfigured

CHAPTER 12

Transfiguration: The Privilege of the Spirit-Filled Life

Transfiguration by growth in the Spirit-filled life is the privilege and should be the goal of every Spirit-filled child of God. Transfiguration, or growth in the life of holiness, is not a separate work of God's grace. Rather, it is the Spirit-guided maturation of the soul in the fullness of the two great acts wrought in the soul of the believer by the Holy Spirit—being born of the Spirit and being filled with the Spirit. Being Spirit-filled is not the final goal of God's work in your soul. You are Spirit-filled that you may be Spirit-transfigured.

You can be Spirit-filled in an instant, but transfiguration is a process of the Spirit. We are sanctified by the infilling of the Spirit so that we may grow into Christlike maturity. Christ's transfiguration on the mountain was not the shining of heaven's light upon Him. It was God's glory radiating from Him. The transfiguration of the Christian is not a halo sent from heaven to crown you. It is a radiance from the holy Trinity indwelling you. It is the radiance of the Father's presence, the Christlikeness of the indwelling Son of God, the glory of the Holy Spirit expressing His natural fruitfulness personalized in your life.

The holy Shekinah, the fiery glory cloud, was removed symbolically from the Old Testament temple just as Ezekiel prophesied (Ezek. 11:22–24). This probably occurred some years before the exile, and it was absent for four hundred years. Ezekiel foresaw in his vision that one day the Shekinah glory would return (43:1–5). This was fulfilled on the Day of Pentecost when the glory came to the upper room and then divided into separate tongues of fire that rested on the head of each one who was filled with the Spirit (Acts 2:2–3). No longer was God's glory indwelling a building; now it was indwelling each consecrated believer. The Shekinah is to be personalized in the life of each sanctified, Spirit-filled believer. Fall on your face before God in wonder, thankfulness, love, and adoration! We are walking on holy ground! Who is sufficient for these things (2 Cor. 2:16)? No one! But our all-sufficient God is longing to fulfill this in your walk with Him in the Spirit-filled life.

Your goal as a Christian is Christlikeness, the Holy Spirit forming the image of Christ within you, transfiguring your daily life, and touching your life with glory. This amazing Bible truth is not just a beautiful poetic statement or figure of speech; it is a true spiritual reality. God means just what He says: we can be transfigured. We must humble ourselves before God and in eager faith appropriate all the grace God has provided for us. Transfiguration into true Christlikeness is for you and me today.

The Spirit's Work Within

The Holy Spirit sheds abroad
   His holy love within my soul
So I can bring new joy to God
   As I adore Him and extol.
His love has filled where once was self;
   His love has fully satisfied.
My hungry heart feasts on His wealth
   Which His abundance has supplied.

How could I be my Savior's bride
   Until the Spirit me prepare,
Till I could stand my God beside
   Adorned with His own graces rare?
Oh, tempt me not with things of earth;
   God's heaven has in me begun.
All else I count as of no worth—
   God now indwells the heart He won!

Each day I more to Him conform;
   Each day I more of grace receive.

His image in me He will form
  As I obey, love, and believe.
The days go oh, so swiftly by
  As for my Bridegroom I prepare.
Each moment brings His coming nigh
  When all His glory I shall share.

The Spirit's fruit I now enjoy;
  The carnal struggle now is past.
His inward peace naught can destroy
  As I explore His grace so vast.
Oh, may He fill me more and more
  And quickly me for Christ prepare.
Soon will I face to face adore
  And wed my Savior in the air.

Wesley L. Duewel

In Matthew 17:1–2 we read of the transfiguration of Jesus Christ, where the Greek word used is *metamorphomai*, the same word used in Romans 12:2, "Be transformed," where it is better translated "transfigured." The word is used of us again in 2 Corinthians 3:18. Why does the Holy Spirit use the same Greek word for Christ's transfiguration as for the transfiguration of Spirit-filled Christians? Why does the Holy Spirit use the same word for the glory of God's presence in believers (2 Cor. 3:18) as for the Shekinah glory of the triune God? Is the glory that shone from between the cherubim in the temple to shine from our unworthy faces when we are Spirit-filled? There can be no other conclusion. Why does the Holy Spirit use the same word for Christ, the image of the invisible God (2 Cor. 4:4), as for us as conformed to the image of Christ (2 Cor. 3:18)?

Why? Because we are to reveal in our lives the image of Christ just as Christ manifested the image of God the Father. When Philip said, "Show us the Father," Jesus could ask, "Don't you know me, Philip? . . . Anyone who has seen me has seen the Father" (John 14:8–10). Can we truly say to people, "Watch my life and you will see the image of Jesus," or, "I am filled with His Spirit, and He is literally transfiguring me into His likeness"? God forgive us if we fail to preach, teach, and manifest the high scriptural standard of the transfiguration of the Spirit-filled believer by the indwelling Holy Spirit. This is the holy life God wants us to experience more and more as we grow in grace after we are Spirit-filled.

The Holy Spirit, the great Teacher (John 16:13), associates together three concepts—our transfiguration, our being conformed to the image of Christ, and God's Shekinah glory in us—as the result of the growth process that occurs after we are filled with the Spirit. As long as bitter roots of our carnal, unsanctified nature exist within us (Heb. 12:15), the sweet, holy image of Christ is marred by our carnality. This is why transfiguration is primarily the process that takes place after our being sanctified by the infilling of the Holy Spirit.

Paul writes, "[You] have put on the new self, which is being renewed in knowledge in the image of its Creator" (Col. 3:10 free translation). We are made into God's very image beginning with an instantaneous crisis experience of sanctification when we receive the fullness of the Holy Spirit and then by the process of transfiguration in which we are continually filled with the Spirit as we hunger and ask (Luke 11:13) and obey God (Acts 5:32). Romans 12:2 tells us not to be conformed to this age but to be transfigured by the renewing of our mind—that is, by the new ideals that mold our mind.

Christ is our ideal. As the indwelling Spirit reveals more and more of Christ's beauty and holiness (for only the pure in heart can really see God—Matt. 5:8; Heb. 12:14) and we thus have a more glorious and complete ideal of Christlikeness before us, we earnestly desire to become more like Him.

As soon as the Holy Spirit conforms our spirit to the new ideal He has set before us, we are capable of a still newer, even fuller revelation of Christ. The Holy Spirit, in His total lordship in our Spirit-filled lives, conforms our eager, yielded spirits to this higher ideal, and we are transfigured step by step, higher and higher into the image of Christ, who is the image of the invisible God (Col. 1:15).

For example, perhaps the Spirit gives you deeper spiritual understanding of Jesus' patience. He prompts you to yearn for your personal patience to be multiplied into all the graciousness, longsuffering patience of Jesus. You pray, "Wonderful Jesus, give me more and more of Your holy patience that my every word, thought, and act demonstrate Your beautiful Spirit-given patience." As a hungering child of God, you are conformed by the Spirit until your life reflects the holy patience of Jesus Himself.

Perhaps the Spirit then gives you, as a maturing Spirit-filled Christian, a new revelation of what Jesus meant when He said, "Learn from me, for I am gentle and humble in heart, and you will find rest for your souls" (Matt. 11:29). Your heart instantly cries out, "Oh, Lord, give me more of Jesus' sweet gentleness. Make my nature gentle and sweet like that of Jesus." You realize more fully what the Holy Spirit meant when He guided Paul to write, "Be completely humble and gentle; be patient, bearing with one another in love" (Eph. 4:2).

As you continue to ask the Lord to build His character in you, the Spirit matures you and makes you more like Jesus and you thus reflect more of God's Shekinah glory. As Proverbs 4:18 says, "The path of the righteous is like the first gleam of dawn, shining ever brighter till the full light of day." And as the Spirit said through Daniel, "Those who are wise will shine like the brightness of the heavens, and those who lead many to righteousness, like the stars for ever and ever" (Dan. 12:3).

The Spirit's goal for you is to make your personality more attractive to Jesus, to make you more radiantly beautiful as His bride. Paul tells us, "Christ loved the church and gave himself up for her to maker her holy . . . and to present her to himself as a radiant church, without stain or wrinkle or any other blemish, but holy and blameless" (Eph. 5:25–27).

In 2 Corinthians 3:16–18 Paul explains our transfiguration even further: "Whenever a person turns [in repentance] to the Lord, the veil is stripped off *and* taken away. Now the Lord is the Spirit, and where the Spirit of the Lord is, there is liberty (emancipation from bondage, freedom). And all of us, as with unveiled face, [because we] continued to behold [in the Word of God] as in a mirror the glory of the Lord, are constantly being transfigured into His *very own* image in ever increasing splendor *and* from one degree of glory to another; [for this comes] from the Lord [Who is] the Spirit" (AMP).

Such growth in grace is purposed by the Spirit and eagerly appropriated by the spiritually healthy Spirit-filled Christian. A desire for Christlikeness has stirred the hearts of many hymn writers. Hear the familiar words of Eliza Hewitt:

More about Jesus would I know,
More of His grace to others show;

More of His saving fullness see,
  More of His love who died for me.

More about Jesus let me learn,
More of His holy will discern;
  Spirit of God, my teacher be,
  Showing the things of Christ to me.

The prayer of Charles Wesley in "Love Divine" is also for Christ-like perfection.

Finish then Thy new creation,
  Pure and spotless let us be;
Let us see Thy great salvation
  Perfectly restored in Thee.
Changed from glory into glory,
  Till in heaven we take our place,
Till we cast our crowns before Thee,
  Lost in wonder, love, and praise.

Thomas Chisholm likewise prayed in "O to Be Like Thee!":

O to be like Thee! blessed Redeemer,
  This is my constant longing and prayer.
Gladly I'll forfeit all of earth's treasures,
  Jesus, Thy perfect likeness to wear.

Chorus:
O to be like Thee! O to be like Thee,
  Blessed Redeemer, pure as Thou art!
Come in Thy sweetness, come in Thy fullness!
  Stamp Thine own image deep on my heart!

How long can this desire to grow in Christ continue? Paul has the answer: "I am convinced *and* sure of this very thing, that He Who began a good work in you will continue until the day of Jesus Christ [right up to the time of His return], developing [that good work] *and* perfecting *and* bringing it to full completion in you" (Phil. 1:6 AMP). The transfiguration process is not to cease until Jesus comes and takes us to Himself at His second coming or takes us through death into final glorification. We shall be like Him, for we shall see Him as He really is in all His transfiguring glory (1 John 3:2). John continues with holy logic, "Everyone who has this hope in him purifies himself, just as he is pure" (v. 3).

The Beauty of Holiness

Beautify Your people, Lord,
  With Your purifying grace.
Now our trusting faith reward
  As we seek Your holy face;
Purify us now, O God,
With the precious cleansing blood.

Take away our carnal traits;
  Fill us with Your perfect love.
Burn up jealousies and hates
  With Your fire from heav'n above.
Set our hearts aglow with light
Shining with Your glory bright.

May the Spirit's lovely fruit—
  Patience, meekness, gentleness—
In our inner selves take root
  Growing into loveliness.
May their flowers in us bloom
Fragrant with Your sweet perfume.

Beautify Your Church, O Lord,
  Till the world is made to see
All the glories of Your Word
  Reproduced in purity.
Help us Your great love express
Beautiful in holiness.

Wesley L. Duewel

CHAPTER 13

Transfiguring Growth: Our Responsibility

We have seen how spiritual transfiguration is held out before us as God's provision for the Spirit-filled person. Since we were created in the image of God so that we could be indwelled by and filled with the Spirit, this is the great desire of God the Father, Son, and Holy Spirit. Yet in full respect of our Godlike free choice, God waits for us to take initiative in the process of transfiguration.

The Holy Spirit took the initiative in revealing God's glorious plan by inspiring the biblical writers. He also takes the initiative in giving us holy hunger to draw near to God. He encourages us by blessing every response we make to His holy drawing. And the more He reveals Christ's love to us, the more we long to be drawn closer to Him. Let us sing with hymn writer Fanny Crosby:

> Oh, the pure delight of a single hour
>   That before Thy throne I spend,
> When I kneel in prayer, and with Thee, my God,
>   I commune as friend with friend!
>
> There are depths of love that I cannot know
>   Till I cross the narrow sea;
> There are heights of joy that I may not reach
>   Till I rest in peace with Thee.
>
> Chorus:
> Draw me nearer, nearer, blessed Lord,
>   To the cross where Thou hast died;
> Draw me nearer, nearer, nearer, blessed Lord,
>   To Thy precious bleeding side.

Fanny J. Crosby

Our hearts cry out to our beloved Lord as in the words of the beloved to her lover in Song of Songs 1:4, "Draw me after you" (NRSV). As He draws us nearer to Himself and we respond with lavish yearning love, we are transfigured by the Spirit in fulfillment of God's gracious promise, "Come near to God and he will come near to you" (James 4:8). We have to agree with Asaph, "As for me, it is good to be near God" (Ps. 73:28).

Peter declared: "[God's] divine power has given us everything we need for life and godliness through our knowledge of him who called us by his own glory and goodness. Through these he has given us his very great and precious promises, so that through them you may participate in the divine nature and escape the corruption in the world caused by evil desires" (2 Peter 1:3–4).

"Participate in" in New Testament Greek is *koinonoi*. We are to be "partners, associates, companions of God" and are to partake and share in God's nature—*phuseos*. Thayer's *Greek-English Lexicon of the New Testament* says of this word, "The holiness distinctive of the divine nature is specially referred to."[1] The Holy Spirit so conforms us to God's holiness that we share in His nature. We are to choose to increase this holy likeness. Our response to the Spirit, our cooperation is described thus: "For this very reason, make every effort to add to your faith goodness; and to goodness, knowledge; and to knowledge, self-control; and to self-control, perseverance; and to perseverance, godliness; and to godliness, brotherly kindness; and to brotherly kindness, love" (2 Peter 1:5–7). Immediately, in the next verse, we are urged to "possess these qualities in increasing measure." In other words, God transfigures us as we respond to the Spirit, follow the Spirit's guidance, and choose to continue to be transfigured.

Think of what God has revealed here in His inspired Word: we can always go deeper in our spiritual life. We can always receive more of God's Spirit-given beauty and glory. And this will assure greater reward in eternity, as God will reward each of His children above and beyond what he or she deserves. Correspondingly greater rewards will be give to all who emphasize loving God, growing in grace, and loving and serving others (1 Cor. 3:11–14).

The more we put Christ's kingdom first here and now, the more Christ will reward us with kingdom blessings in eternity. Whatever we do out of love for Jesus, whatever we do to please Him, whatever we do now to glorify Him and extend His kingdom will be lavishly rewarded by God in eternity. Since these rewards will last forever, we can do nothing wiser, more rewarding, and more sure of multiplied spiritual benefits. God in His inexhaustible wisdom will have ever new, ever more blessed ways to reveal His loving goodness to us, and ever more holy surprises of His grace, love, and power.

The glorious revelations that God will share with us and the joy-filled events He has planned for us to share in will keep on unfolding as eternal days succeed each other. Our present human vocabulary is too limited to begin to describe the glories God has waiting for us. Heaven's vocabulary alone is capable of describing all that God is planning for those who love Him. Paul makes brief mention of this in 2 Corinthians 12:1–4. God permitted him for brief moments to be so spiritually enraptured that he was not sure whether he was "in the body or apart from the body." Paul experienced a heavenly snatching away from his normal environment and was suddenly transported to paradise, where he heard "inexpressible things, things that man is not permitted to tell."

The same Greek word is used of the Spirit's instant snatching away of Paul to the third heaven (2 Cor. 12:2), as is used of the Spirit's snatching up of Philip from the Gaza road and transporting him to Ashdod (also called Azotus) miles away (Acts 8:39–40). The same word is also used in 1 Thessalonians 4:17 to describe how Jesus will rapture, or snatch up, His saints from normal earth living into His presence "in the air." Clearly, this is an instantaneous, joyous, glory-filled moment when our earthly body will be transformed to a spiritual body (1 Cor. 15:44) that can experience thereafter the eternal joys and glories of heaven.

Why did God plan this glorious but momentary foretaste of what will be blessedly natural to us in eternity? He wanted us to have a momentary glimpse of heaven and its glories so that we would be assured of how richly wonderful these spiritual realities are. But heaven's glories will not be experienced the same way by all.[2] Although all Christians will be in the same heaven, not all believers are now developing their spiritual capacities to the same extent here. Many are failing to prepare their souls for the glory of eternity.

Will not all Christians receive glorified bodies in heaven? Most certainly they will. But there will be a definite reward-relation between the closeness and carefulness of our walk with

God here and the blessedness of our role and experience in heaven. We will have personal and differing inheritances in heaven, just as we have differing degrees of participating in spiritual kingdom blessings here.

God's blessings are equally available for appropriation by our faith and obedience. Growth in grace results not by divine fiat but by personal appropriation. God's provisions of grace are available for all but are not equally hungered for or taken possession of by all. Just as Mary chose what is better (to sit at Jesus' feet) and Jesus said it would not be taken from her (Luke 10:42), so our choosing right spiritual priorities now will have eternal resulting blessings that will never be lost or taken from us.

We must make use of spiritual opportunities while we have them, even as Mary chose to sit at Jesus' feet. Seize opportunities for growth in grace while you have them. Choose to give priority to developing the fruit of the Spirit. Choose to develop your prayer life. You must choose if you would make growth your priority.

Peter's prayer in 2 Peter 1:2 was that his readers would be given "grace and peace . . . in abundance." Thus, in verses 5–7 he urges us to add one godly virtue to another, emphasizing the urgency to grow so that we "possess these qualities in increasing measure" (literally, so that we "superabound" in them). Then we will not be "ineffective and unproductive" (v. 8). He urges us to "make every effort" to add goodness, knowledge, self-control, perseverance, godliness, brotherly kindness, and love. He exhorts us not to be content with our spiritual life but to continually add the fruit of the Spirit.

If we understood eternity as the Holy Spirit does, we would make producing the fruit of the Spirit our holy priority. Nothing is more urgent nor more rewarding eternally. This is why He has provided for us to be Spirit-filled now here on earth. He wants our eternal days to be as glorious as possible. Don't miss all that God the Father longs to give you throughout eternity— grace beyond grace and glory beyond glory.

These are the qualifying days, the seed-sowing days. Eternity will be the redemption days, the glorious reaping days. God has a harvest of glory planned for you. He is keeping you alive so that you can grow more and more like Jesus. Don't miss what God wants to give you by failing to give priority to being transfigured by the Spirit into ever-increasing Christlikeness.

CHAPTER 14

Radiant Lives and Faces

Some of God's saintly children have not only gone from glory to glory in holy Christlikeness of personality (2 Cor. 3:18), but God has so indwelt them that their lives and even their faces have become at times radiant from His presence. We should not be surprised that those who draw very near to God and live in utmost fellowship, intimacy, and communion with Him sometimes reflect on their faces the radiant glory of our ascended Lord. Just as Jesus, God's Son, is the radiance of God's glory (Heb. 1:3), so we can with unveiled faces "reflect the Lord's glory" as we "are being transformed into his likeness with ever-increasing glory, which comes from the Lord, who is the Spirit" (2 Cor. 3:18).

David said, "Those who look to him are radiant" (Ps. 34:5). The Holy Spirit is pleased to give touches of His beauty and radiance as a visible seal of His love, approval, and identity with us.

Moses

Even in Old Testament days Moses drew so close to God in spirit that God permitted him to climb Mount Sinai while it was covered with the awesome Shekinah fire of God. Moses so loved and adored God and so hungered to know Him more intimately that by God's command he came closer to the manifestation of God's fiery glory than any human being had ever come. Read of his holy hunger in Exodus 33:12–23 and 34:5–10.

Moses met with God within the glory fire twice, forty days each time. He was supernaturally protected, sustained, and preserved by God's gracious presence. He neither ate nor drank, yet he was kept alive, strong and well. Moses entered the cloud of God's manifested presence and was "face to face" with Him (Ex. 33:11; Deut. 34:10).

When Moses came down after the eighty days with God, he did not realize that his face was aglow with the radiance of God that had saturated his being (Ex. 34:29–35). Stephen may have had a radiance of this kind as he stood before the Sanhedrin, for Scripture says, "His face was like the face of an angel" (Acts 6:15). And to a lesser degree, some of the same beauty is at times glimpsed on the faces of God's children today.

Savonarola

During the spiritually dark days before the Reformation, Savonarola was a saint and martyr for Christ. He knew a greater part of the Bible by memory, and he often spent entire nights in prayer and days in fasting and prayer. He fearlessly preached the Gospel and condemned sin. God gave him unusual prophecies that were accurately fulfilled and through him sent a mighty eight-year revival to Florence, Italy. At times when Savonarola preached, a divine light seemed to beam from his eyes and shine from his face.[1]

George Whitefield

When George Whitefield, mighty evangelist in the days of John Wesley, preached to thousands, he often would begin to weep before he finished preaching. At times he was "radiant with the light from heaven," and the eyes of many would be riveted on him.[2]

John Fletcher

John Fletcher, godly coworker of John Wesley, a man constantly engaged in fasting and prayer, was known for his holy life. Wesley called him the holiest man he ever knew. When he was president of Trevecca College, students would lay aside everything to hear him speak. He told them over and over that to be filled with the Spirit was more important than all their studies, and he spent hours on his knees praying for them to be filled. Once while praying, Fletcher was so overwhelmed with the Spirit's love and power that he cried out, "Oh, my God, withhold Thy hand, or the vessel will burst."[3]

Charles G. Finney

Charles G. Finney, one of the greatest soul-winning evangelists since Pentecost, lived in constant awareness of God's presence. One day as he neared the church where he was to preach, "a light perfectly ineffable" shone in his soul and almost prostrated him on the ground. It seemed to him brighter than the noonday sun. He learned to travail mightily in prayer, and many were saved and some were healed in answer to his prayers.

Sometimes when Finney preached, nearly the entire audience fell on their knees in prayer, and "at times . . . the power of the Spirit seemed to descend like a cloud of glory upon him."[4]

Jonathan Goforth

Jonathan Goforth, a Canadian Presbyterian missionary a century ago, was a Spirit-filled man of God who was mightily used in revival in China. One of his friends said there was always a sense of the Lord's presence coming from him.[5] Another said, "He was one who walked with God" and added that his every word and act seemed to radiate the sense of God's presence. "I remember having the same blessed realization when in the presence of Dr. Hudson Taylor and Dr. A. J. Gordon and one or two besides."[6]

A Toronto businessman said of Goforth, "His religion and his love for helping others shone in his face."[7] Another friend reported that "it was a joy even to look at him, for his radiant face was a true witness of the words, 'To me to live is Christ.'"[8] One Chinese man said that it was impossible to look in his face and not love and believe in him.[9]

In the latter part of his life, Goforth was blind. He gave his last message in Toronto. "As Mr. McPherson led Dr. Goforth into the pulpit, he walked with firm steps, head erect, and face aglow with the joy of Christ; the sightless eyes were turned upward as if he could see. The congregation listened with marked attention and stillness as with radiant joy, as seeing the Lord he loved, he delivered his address (on revival in Korea) in the power of the Spirit." Many present spoke of the radiance of his face as he spoke. At seven o'clock the next morning he died in his sleep, and the next face he saw was Jesus.[10]

Duncan Campbell

On one occasion when Rev. Duncan Campbell, a dear friend of mine in Scotland, came down from the pulpit to baptize a person, the glory of God shone so brightly on his face that an ex-army lieutenant sitting below could hardly look at him. A few hours later the lieutenant was wonderfully saved as Mr. Campbell prayed.[11]

On several occasions during Campbell's ministry, others were gripped by the glory of God on his face. At times some of his students in the Faith Mission Bible College hesitated to look up at his face because they sensed so much of God's presence in him. One night in Aberdare, Scotland, six young men sitting together saw "the glory of God" come down upon him as he preached. They fell to the floor weeping. God gripped the congregation, and person after person repented and made restitution that night.[12]

Robert Murray M'Cheyne

Scotland's beloved Robert Murray M'Cheyne longed, "Oh, for closest communion with God, till soul and body—head, face, and heart—shine with Divine brilliancy! But oh! for a holy ignorance of our shining!"[13]

After M'Cheyne's death a letter came from one who heard his last sermon. "I hope you will pardon a stranger for addressing to you a few lines. I heard you preach last Sabbath evening, and it pleased God to bless that sermon to my soul. It was not so much what you said as your manner of speaking, that struck me. I saw in you a beauty of holiness that I never saw before."[14]

Dr. D. Martyn Lloyd-Jones has said:

When the church is in a state of revival, you do not have to exhort people to praise; you cannot stop them, they are so filled with God. Their very faces show it. They are transfigured. There is a heavenly look that comes upon their faces, which is expressive of this joy, this praise. Can we not see that this is the need of the church today? . . . When the Holy Ghost has fallen, people are filled with this joy. It is not a superficial, carnal, put-on thing, it is a thing that comes from within; the power of the Spirit irradiating the whole personality, and giving a joy which is "unspeakable, and full of glory."[15]

God does not promise to manifest His glory visibly, and we should not pray for spectacular visible manifestations of God's power or glory. But at times, perhaps for brief moments, God grants His hungry-hearted followers a brief touch of His visible glory. They are not seeking it and like Moses are unaware of what others see. They are selflessly humble. They delight in the Lord, yearn for more of Him, and are devoted to prayer and serving God. Then just when they are hungriest for more of God, unknown to them, God lets His hidden presence in their hearts be sweetly seen on their face. The following poem expresses this very manifestation.

Indwelt

Not merely in the words you say,
    Not only in your deeds confessed,
But in the most unconscious way
    Is Christ expressed!

For me 'twas not the truth you taught
    To you so clear, to me still dim,
But when you came to me you brought
    A sense of Him.

And from your eyes He beckons me
    And from your heart His love is shed,
Till I lose sight of you—and see
    The Christ instead.

Anonymous

CHAPTER 15

Empowering and Anointing by the Spirit

The Holy Spirit delights in pouring His power through believers again and again and in increasing measure. God cannot trust His power to an unsurrendered, uncrucified, unsanctified heart. Only the cleansed can be empowered in the fullest sense. The Spirit's anointing abides in us (1 John 2:27) to empower, equip, teach, and use us gloriously and miraculously. He abides within us and is available at any moment to provide what we need. Oh, how we have neglected to teach and preach the role of repeated anointings through the Spirit who fills us!

Many godly people seem so often to testify, preach, write, teach, or perform other acts of Christian service without fresh anointing. Instead, they rely on their own knowledge, skill, and experience. But anyone who has had the anointing of God knows the difference it makes in ministering and in the results of ministry. Spirit-filled singers, musicians, teachers, writers—all believers—can know the Holy Spirit's anointing, which adds an extra and special dimension to whatever one is doing. He touches our thinking, our emotions, and our skills, aptness, and effectiveness. A godly surgeon once told me he knew when his surgery was anointed and when it wasn't.

The Holy Spirit's anointing is not a one-time experience. When persons are totally consecrated and have been cleansed and filled with the Spirit, they can be refilled, reanointed, and specially touched repeatedly. This is what we should long for and pray for every time we minister. God forgive us for our willingness to serve without fresh anointing and adequate prayer preparation.

Charles G. Finney testified that if he sensed the lack of God's power and results for a day or two in his ministry, he immediately resorted to fasting and prayer for two or three days, and invariably he again felt the mighty hand of God upon him and the revival continued in power. Many today write, teach, and minister and hardly ever sense God's powerful anointing for their work. Thus, it is not surprising that the church sees so little supernatural growth today.

Woe to us if we seek after the Holy Spirit's gifts rather than after the Holy Giver! Those who are Spirit-filled, Spirit-transfigured, Spirit-empowered, and Spirit-anointed need not hunger for spectacular gifts, for they have the Giver Himself, who is greater than all His gifts. He gives His own whatever they need to do God's will. Since anointing is not a separate, new work of grace in the soul, but rather is part of the spiritual inheritance and privilege of those who are Spirit-filled, those who are walking in the light need only to ask and receive as often as they like (Luke 11:13). We are free to ask for each new occasion. Constantly hunger and ask for new, fresh anointing if you long to be constantly anointed.

Fill Me Again

Fill me again and again, dear Lord;
    Fill with Your Spirit just now.
Trusting Your promise, Your holy Word,
    Thirsting and waiting I bow.
More of Your Spirit is what I need—
More of Your Spirit in me, I plead.
Fulfill Your mission, yes, quickly speed!
    Fill me again, my God.

Reign absolutely on my heart's throne;
    Fill me and use me again.
Let all Your ministry now be known;
    Meet through my life needs of men.
Fill me till others lose sight of me;
Fill me till others Your image see.
Fill me and flood me like waves of the sea.
    Fill me again, my God!

Spirit of God fill me constantly;
    Fill with Your own holiness.

Fill me and use me increasingly;
　Fill with Your sweet loveliness.
Fill with anointing and holy pow'r;
Fill me and use me, Lord, hour by hour.
Hungerings for You my whole soul devour!
　Fill me again, my God.

Not for Your gifts do I hunger now;
　It is for You that I cry.
O Triune God, at Your feet I bow—
　You can my soul satisfy!
Fill me more fully than e'er before;
Fill and refill my soul o'er and o'er.
I long for more of You, more and more!
　Fill me again, my God!

Wesley L. Duewel

The Holy Spirit longs to prove His presence by a thousand workings within you and through you as a Spirit-filled believer. He proves His presence by the fruit of the Spirit given in holy abundance—love, joy, peace, longsuffering—rivers of living water flowing out from your innermost being in holy floods of blessing (John 7:38–39; Gal. 5:22–23). The Holy Spirit can guide you again and again in prayer at the exact time someone has a particular need. He will guide you in speech and in action to minister to prepared hearts, to win souls, to be used in revival. He will anoint you as often as you ask so that you sing in the Spirit, write in the Spirit, preach in the Spirit, pray in the Spirit, and literally live in the Spirit.

The Spirit's Presence

Jesus expects us, His disciples, to make a difference in our world by our loving, witnessing lives, our powerful praying, and our demonstration of His power and authority. Jesus promised His followers, "You will receive power when the Holy Spirit comes on you; and you will be my witnesses" (Acts 1:8). Above all else, we must receive the enablement of the Spirit to be equipped for witnessing. That is why Jesus said, "You are witnesses," and then added, "I am going to send you what my Father has promised; but stay in the city [Jerusalem] until you have been clothed with power from on high" (Luke 24:48–49). "First," Jesus says, "receive My power, then be My witnesses. Wait here until you are filled with that power." Because Jesus loved His disciples and knew the kind of people to whom they would witness, He did not want them to try to serve Him until they were spiritually ready.

Being filled with the Spirit's power is not an optional luxury. It is vital if you and I are to represent Him. How can you and I represent God? Only if we are first made holy and then filled and anointed with a power to be all He wants us to be and to do all He wants us to do. We must be Spirit-equipped to be ambassadors for Christ (2 Cor. 5:20).

The power of the Spirit is first of all the power to live a holy life, to be victorious in temptation, to daily manifest the fruit of the Spirit. The Spirit-filled person is empowered to be Christlike. In Him, the holy love of 1 Corinthians 13 is demonstrated in Spirit-filled living.

In the words of Paul, the love of a cleansed, holy heart is patient, is kind, does not envy, does not boast, is not proud. It is not rude, is not self-seeking. Sanctified love is not provoked, keeps no record of wrongs, does not delight in evil but rejoices with the truth. Holy love always protects, always trusts, always hopes, always perseveres. It never fails (1 Cor. 13:4–8; for a fuller description see the appendix).

The power of the Spirit is what keeps us holy and loving in all our reactions, relationships, and emotions. It is the Spirit's power alone that never fails. Provocations are sure to come to everyone. There is no greater testimony to the reality of being cleansed from all sin and filled with the Holy Spirit than when other people see nothing but pure love in our reactions and when we experience nothing but pure loving sweetness in our innermost nature.

This power to be holy in heart is more important than the power to do miracles or to manifest any or all of the gifts of the Spirit. But His power is also our divine enabling in speech, in prayer, and in all of our obedience and serving under the Spirit's leadership. We can have the Spirit's empowering touch on our public reading of the Word; on our private or public praying; on our witnessing, teaching, speaking, preaching, and singing; and on our blessing others in any way. It is God's seal to us and to others. People, especially those with spiritual discernment, sense that God is specially present and using us for His holy purposes. The anointing identifies God's presence with us and authority upon us.

We cannot bring the Holy Spirit's anointing down upon ourselves. That is, it is not dependent upon or brought about by our loudness or softness of voice or by our gestures. It is almost impossible to define yet blessedly evident. It may be accompanied by a holy hush as we recognize that God is specially with us or speaking to us, that God is using our efforts, that God is graciously near us. Or it may be a sense of holy power and authority as we speak or pray in His name.

May God be pleased to grant us repeatedly His gracious and powerful anointing, the awareness that He is with us. John Wesley had experienced the anointing so many times that on his deathbed he recognized it again, and his dying words were, "The best of all is God is with us." Oh, the blessedness of the anointing ministry of the Spirit.

A powerful life of prevailing intercessory prayer is also practical evidence of one's sharing Christ's heartbeat of redemptive love for the unsaved for whom He died, for a world so in need of His touch, and for the church, Christ's bride. How mightily God can anoint Spirit-filled persons and give them freedom and faith as they intercede in prayer. And what astounding answers God can give to Spirit-led and Spirit-empowered prevailing in prayer.

Only rarely does God shake a location literally and physically as He did when the apostles prayed in Acts 4:31. Spiritually, however, God has shaken places again and again in answer to prevailing prayer. Most of us have never really given ourselves to God regularly in prayer that truly prevails before God and prevails over all the resistance of Satan and hell. God forgive us for knowing so little of the empowering of the Spirit in our private prayer times and in our public and pulpit praying. We are depriving God's people of the Spirit-anointed leading in prayer that God wants us to manifest.

May God help us as Spirit-filled people to give ourselves to Spirit-anointed praying. Many things will continue to hinder God's purposes until His church prevails. When we do put prayer first, however, God will be pleased and His holy will will be fulfilled. Modern-day Sauls can become God's Pauls for our generation. Hearts closed to gospel power can be opened wide to the Spirit when we engage in spiritual travail. Long-awaited revival can come when we meet God's covenant conditions in 2 Chronicles 7:14.

Lord, teach us to humble ourselves before You in mighty Spirit-empowered prevailing intercession.

CHAPTER 16

Shekinah Glory upon the Spirit-Filled

In the Old Testament, one of the symbols of the Holy Spirit and one of the evidences of God's presence was the cloud of fire, or the glory cloud, often called the Shekinah. It was first manifested to Moses at the burning bush and later led Israel out of Egypt into Canaan. It was manifested at the top of Mount Sinai when God gave the Ten Commandments, and it remained between the cherubim on the cover of the ark of the covenant and was thus resident in the Holy of Holies. The Shekinah was always very meaningful to Israel, assuring them that God was with them.

Ezekiel saw God's glory cloud departing from the temple in a vision, symbolizing that God's presence was leaving backsliding Judah. Ezekiel saw the cloud first leave the Holy of Holies and stop at the door of the temple (Ezek. 9:3; 10:4). The people should have heeded this warning but instead continued to backslide. Then the Shekinah rose and went to the east of the temple area (10:18–19). Next it left the city of Jerusalem completely and tarried above the Mount of Olives east of the city. Later Ezekiel had a vision of the time when the Shekinah would return (43:1–3).

For some four hundred years God's glory cloud was absent. Jesus said, "Your house is left to you desolate" (Matt. 23:38). In other words, He was saying, "It used to be My temple. Now I have withdrawn the symbol of My presence and left the house to you. I am no longer there." Ezekiel's vision of the Shekinah's return was fulfilled on the Day of Pentecost as the 120 disciples and apostles waited in prayer in an upper room in Jerusalem. First, God alerted Jerusalem and the disciples by the sound of a rushing mighty wind. Since then God has only rarely done this in revival. When God sent the sound of rushing wind at a Dutch Reformed Church in South Africa, Rev. Andrew Murray at first did not know how to react. But then he recognized that it was the presence of God. God worked graciously in revival.

Then when God had the attention of those in the upper room, He fulfilled Ezekiel's vision. Ezekiel had seen the glory cloud return in the eastern sky. Now at Pentecost it appeared again. It entered the upper room and separated and rested on the head of each of them when they were filled with the Spirit (Acts 2:1–4, 38–39). Previously the Shekinah had been one whole; now in the New Testament age the manifestation was primarily to be personalized. Rather than dwelling in a sacred building, the Shekinah would be manifest in the life and ministry of Spirit-filled people. Today only rarely is it seen as a visible glory and fire.

The Holy Spirit's presence is basically invisible to our human eye. It cannot be adequately imitated or put on as some external holiness. But as recorded in biographies of godly Christians or accounts of revivals, God has on occasion been pleased to put a visible seal upon His children. A biblical example of this is the face of Stephen (Acts 6:15). When the Sanhedrin looked intently at his face, they saw it was "like the face of an angel."

God Puts His Seal on John Wesley

Biographers record that several men once stood on the edge of a crowd with stones in their hands, which they intended to hurl at John Wesley. They were so overawed by the presence of God in him that one by one the stones fell on the ground as their eyes were riveted on his face. And one man said to the other, "He's not a man! He's not a man!" He was a man, but the Spirit of God was resting upon him and evident in his face.

God Blesses with His Presence

During the 1920s my father pastored a Methodist Church in Nashville, Illinois. God sent revival to two of the local churches during that time. A weekly afternoon Bible study was held in the home of a Mrs. Hiser, a Spirit-filled, gifted Bible teacher. Among those who attended the Bible studies were four of the pastors of the local churches and their wives. The pastors of the Baptist church, the Presbyterian church, and two of the Methodist churches had all experienced the fullness of the Holy Spirit. I remember Mother telling what blessed times they had in the Bible studies as they meditated on the deep truths of God's Word.

Mother told me of one afternoon when their Bible study subject was heaven. While they were meditating together that afternoon, the electric light in the room seemed to change to an almost heavenly light and brightness. No one mentioned anything at the time, but several days later one of the pastors' wives met my mother in the grocery store. As they talked, the woman said, "Sister Duewel, when we were studying about heaven the other afternoon, did you notice anything unusual about the light?"

"Yes," my mother answered quietly, "I saw it too."

Why would God draw so near with an unusual awareness of His presence? No one expected or asked for such a manifestation of the loving presence of God, and it was not repeated. It was simply a fulfillment of James 4:8, "Come near to God and he will come near to you."

In that same town, I, as a five-year-old boy playing alone in the sandbox, had a sudden clear call to be a missionary to India. I heard no voice and saw no vision, but the call was impressed upon my heart so suddenly, clearly, and unmistakably that seventy-eight years later I cannot deny or doubt.

God Responds to a Hunger for His Presence

A Spirit-filled Bible college student came home for summer vacation. He was living close to the Lord, spending considerable time in prayer for revival and missionary harvest and longing for more of God's presence in his life. His father pastored a small church and received only a meager salary. One member of the church had a cow, and if the young man's mother would take over an empty half-gallon milk pail, the generous church member would fill it with milk and send it back.

One day the student was sent to the church member's home to get a pail of milk. As he walked down the street with the empty pail, he was so lost in prayer, hungering for more of God's presence, he hardly saw where he was walking. Arriving at the home, he found the housewife washing clothes at the washing machine on the far side of the kitchen.

The pail was filled with milk, and the youth was ready to leave but suggested that they have a word of prayer before he went on his way. Kneeling down, he began to pray. The housewife was very agreeable and knelt down as the young man asked God's blessing on the home. He then excused himself and left.

An unsaved relative from another city, who was visiting there, was in the kitchen at the time. After the youth had gone, the visiting woman asked, in awe, "Who was that? I just felt I wanted to touch him." Unknown to the youth, God's presence had so covered him that the woman was gripped with awe by the Holy Spirit. Out of respect for God's presence, she wanted to reach out and touch him. She didn't know why or how, but she was very aware that God had been present in the room.

God Manifests His Presence

While Rev. Duncan Campbell was principal of the Faith Mission Bible College in Edinburgh, Scotland, Friday mornings were given to prayer and waiting upon God. On March 4, 1960, during such a time of waiting in prayer, God's power came upon the entire assembly. One student told how she did not dare to look up at Rev. Campbell, for she felt that if she looked on his face, she would see God. The group began to sing "Jesus, Keep Me Near the Cross." A number wept tears of joy as "wave after wave of the Spirit's power" was experienced by the group. "Then heavenly music was heard which seemed to fill the room above which they were kneeling; it was indescribably beautiful and harmonious, such as no orchestra could symphonize. This phenomenon was not new to Duncan; at least twice during the Lewis Awakening he had heard celestial melodies. Once in the early hours of the morning, as he was walking through a glen, the heavens seemed to be filled with angelic praise, and two hundred church members walking together dropped to their knees. Another minister present cried out for joy: 'This is heaven! This is heaven!'"[1]

One day during the 1964 Spiritual Life Convention in Lisburn, Northern Ireland, Campbell went to his room to pray after breakfast. The convention chairman was sitting alone in the dining room when he suddenly sensed "the brightness of the presence of the Lord" in the room. He was so overawed by God's presence and felt so unworthy to be in the room that he went out the door. It seemed like the same brightness was filling nature there. He began to weep and turned around and went back into the building. Just then Duncan entered the room, his face "aglow," and told how God had just been with him and was going to send revival.

All day long God's presence seemed to envelop the area. "That evening Duncan preached his final address and pronounced the benediction when, as one person present said: 'God took over the service.' The organist attempted to play but her hands were powerless to touch the keyboard. The whole congregation was 'gripped by an awe-filled stillness so that no one moved for over half an hour. Then some began to pray and weep.'" God worked deeply, and afterward four people reported hearing indescribable sounds from heaven during the holy stillness.[2]

Unusual Power in Prayer

Sometimes God's presence is felt as special power that seems to clothe the words of prayer. At times in India, the great missionary John Hyde, known as Praying Hyde, who lived in an atmosphere of prayer, would call out during a prayer meeting, "O heavenly Father." God's power would seem to descend upon the gathering from just those few words.

As Hyde returned from India to America, he stopped for a few weeks in the British Isles. Dr. J. Wilbur Chapman, who had been mightily used by God in evangelistic campaigns across America and around the world, was in a campaign that was proving to be almost fruitless, with poor attendance and little result. Praying Hyde heard about this and, with much prayer, went to the campaign. That night the hall was packed and fifty men were converted.

Chapman asked Praying Hyde to pray for him. They went to Chapman's hotel room, where Hyde immediately dropped to his knees. For five minutes he did not say a word. Then he called out, "Oh, God." For another five minutes he was absolutely silent, the tears streaming down his face. Again he called out, "Oh, God." Then a torrent of prayer poured from his mouth as he prayed for Chapman and his ministry. Chapman said he had never heard such petitions in prayer in his life, and Chapman went on with new strength and power in his ministry for the Lord. For one week Hyde stayed in the city, praying for Chapman and his campaign, and thereafter Hyde followed Chapman's ministry around the world with prayer.[3]

How often God has used Spirit-anointed prayers of Spirit-filled people to touch heaven's throne and bring remarkable victories for God.

The holy seal of the Lord's presence may rest on individuals or on gatherings of God's children. During revival times God occasionally blesses His people with an unusual awareness of His presence. This manifestation cannot be produced by humans. It cannot be worked up, nor can it be earned. It is not just emotion, though a blessed awareness of God's presence may be sensed. It may be in the form of a holy hush or in the form of holy joy and a spirit of praise. It may be in the form of a prayerful burden and tears. God is sovereign and will manifest His presence in Spirit-filled believers in a way that will bless them and bring glory to Him.

CHAPTER 17

Living in Communing Love

God wants us to live in lavish, outgoing love, goodness, and holiness. He wants those about us to see and feel our loving goodwill in our cheerful helpfulness and expressions of graciousness, thoughtfulness, holiness, and loving concern.

A clear, sparkling stream of holy love flows from the heart of Christ into your heart as a Spirit-filled person and then out of your personality to others. He expresses His love as fully as the spiritual depth of your heart permits. Christ rejoices when you are so holy and loving that He can express through you the otherwise humanly inexpressible love of His heart.

Only as you come very close to Christ do you begin to experience the depths of His divine love. Our bodies, bound by the limitations of our humanity, can barely begin to experience the boundless dimensions of Christ's love. The joy, the yearning, and the immensity of Christ's love would overwhelm us and bring instant death to our frail earthly bodies. But God has planned a new spiritual, glorified body for us in our resurrection state in heaven that will be able to comprehend the love of God in dimensions we have never dreamed possible. But even so, it will still be only a finite comprehension of the infinite love of Christ's heart (Rom. 8:18–20; 1 Cor. 2:4; Rev. 21:10–11; 22:4). Only the Father, Son, and Holy Spirit are capable of receiving that love from each other and reveling in it to the full. Only they will be able to fully comprehend and reciprocate in blessed, infinite fullness of divine love.

The extent of our love commitment to Christ today will set the initial limits of our perception and experience of God's love when we first reach eternity. We were created with the capacity for spiritual growth. I don't doubt that we will experience eternal growth in our perception and experience of God's love and all His holy attributes, but we will still be finite, glorified human creatures. And I expect that our response to Christ's love before death will somehow set the limits of our eternal growth in experiencing and rejoicing in the infinite love of our heavenly Bridegroom.

Note well that God listens to our expressions of love in our prayers and in our conversation with others who are walking close to God.

> Then those who feared the LORD talked with each other, and the LORD listened and heard. A scroll of remembrance was written in his presence concerning those who feared the LORD and honored his name. "They will be mine," says the LORD Almighty, "in the day when I make up my treasured possession. I will spare them, just as in compassion a man spares his son who serves him. And you will again see the distinction between the righteous and the wicked, between those who serve God and those who do not." (Mal. 3:16–18)

How often does God hear you telling others how much you love Him?

The prophet Malachi, speaking of this present age before the return in glory of our Savior, pointed out that some people will be sorcerers, adulterers, perjurers, liars, and people who oppress the poor and helpless and do not live with the fear of God (Mal. 3:5). God will come suddenly in judgment to such people (vv. 1–5). The only reason sinful humanity still continues on earth today is the unfailing mercy of the Lord. That is the one reason hypocritical and unfaithful people who claim to follow God are still alive (v. 6). It is at such a time when millions rob God of their tithes and offerings (vv. 8–12) and others say harsh things against God, claiming it does not benefit a person to serve God (vv. 13–15), that God speaks a promise to those who are truly His own: "Then those who feared the LORD talked with each other, and the LORD listened and heard" (v. 16). All the time a scroll of remembrance was being written in God's presence, recording the prayers and conversations of those who loved Him and honored His name. "'They will be mine,' says the LORD Almighty" (v. 17). God will keep them close to His heart and will love and shelter them. Can you hear God's holy pride as He says that others will see how He rewards, honors, and cherishes His own (v. 18)?

Here, in the second to last chapter of the Old Testament, we see how God treasures every loving thought and word we express about Him. Note that those who love the Lord not only talk to Him in prayer but talk about Him among themselves. This so pleases the Lord that He listens with obvious delight and commands that a scroll of remembrance be written in His presence to record all thoughts, words, and actions of His children. No records anywhere else in the universe are so complete as the records kept in heaven of the deeds—both good and evil—of human beings. These records will enable God to be absolutely fair on Judgment Day when He determines punishment for sinners and rewards for His children.

The Hebrew word *hᵃshab* (KJV "thought," NIV "honored") in Malachi 3:16 means to think, plan, or meditate. So God will reward those who think about Him, meditate on Him, and make their plans in the light of His will. Furthermore, He will have compassion on them, be merciful to them, and spare them in His own wonderful ways. God's special care and loving concern for them will be evident to everyone, and people and angels alike will see how beautifully God honors and rewards throughout eternity those who have proved their love to Him in these ways. Beware lest you become so absorbed in the newspaper, television, and life about you that you neglect to commune with Him, express your love to Him, and feast and meditate each day on His Word and His love.

Is God's record of your loving thoughts and longings for Him a full and extensive one? Are you constantly expressing your love to Him? Nothing is more natural to a Spirit-filled person than to think and talk about the Lord, for a Spirit-filled heart naturally expresses its joy and love. Ephesians 5:18–20 says: "Be filled with the Spirit. Speak to one another with psalms, hymns and spiritual songs. Sing and make music in your heart to the Lord, always giving thanks to God the Father for everything, in the name of our Lord Jesus Christ."

The Spirit-filled person also naturally expresses inner joy and fellowship with Christ in a lifestyle of overflowing love and serving others. Colossians 3:15–17 speaks of this type of love.

Let the peace of Christ rule in your hearts, since as members of one body you were called to peace. And be thankful. Let the word of Christ dwell in you richly as you teach and admonish one another with all wisdom, and as you sing psalms, hymns and spiritual songs with gratitude in your hearts to God. And whatever you do, whether in word or deed, do it all in the name of the Lord Jesus, giving thanks to God the Father through him.

Note that both the Ephesians and Colossians passages speak of singing to the Lord. Just as human lovers thrill to hear their beloved speak their love, so Jesus delights to hear us sing to Him and to tell Him over and over how much we love Him. Be sure to emphasize not only songs that speak *about* His love but also choruses and hymns that express personal love *to* Him. There is great spiritual joy in telling Jesus how much we love Him, and it is also a vital part of our growing in grace.

We need to live in communion with Jesus in our heart and in fellowship with God's children so that we will be strengthened for those times when Satan attacks. Peter cautions:

In this you greatly rejoice, though now for a little while you may have had to suffer grief in all kinds of trials. These have come so that your faith—of greater worth than gold, which perishes even though refined by fire—may be proved genuine and may result in praise, glory and honor when Jesus Christ is revealed. Though you have not seen him, you love him; and even though you do not see him now, you believe in him and are filled with an inexpressible and glorious joy, for you are receiving the goal of your faith, the salvation of your souls. (1 Peter 1:6–9)

The carnal heart out of communion with the Lord often fills its meditation and memory with negative thoughts, critical feelings, grumblings, complainings, suspicions, bitterness, and accusations against others. Is this true of you? Certainly these are not the kinds of thoughts or words with which we want our heavenly record filled.

How different are the Spirit-filled! As they keep thirsting and believing (John 7:37–39), the Holy Spirit fills and refills their souls with such spiritual refreshment that from within them streams (vv. 37–38) of Holy Spirit water flow.

What streams? Streams of Holy Spirit fruitfulness. Streams of love, joy, peace, patience, kindness, goodness, faithfulness, gentleness, and self-control. This is the beautiful life of the Spirit-filled. How refreshing to have Spirit-filled friends, Spirit-filled neighbors, a Spirit-filled pastor, and a church filled with fellowshiping, Spirit-filled people.

Youth, mature Christians, and aged Christians—all can be Spirit-filled and all will show the same beautiful fruit of the Spirit in their lives. All will have a profusion of holy blessings streaming from their happy hearts. I am reminded of the account of a missionary reading to some natives from Paul's epistles. As he read a description of a Spirit-beautified life, the people interrupted him. "Oh, we know him. He comes here every month." What a testimony to someone's Spirit-filled life!

How deeply are you experiencing the blessedness of Jesus' heart? How fully have you known the glory of His transfiguring grace? Let us draw closer to Jesus than we ever have before. Let us plunge more deeply, more daringly than ever before into the blessed ocean of His goodness and His engulfing love for us.

CHAPTER 18

Living in Practical Expressions of Love

The Holy Spirit desires to transfigure us into the spiritual likeness of Jesus. Could there be any greater honor or destiny? The wonderful salvation made possible when Jesus took our place and died for us at Calvary has made all of us who trust in Him for salvation children of God. That is almost unbelievably glorious. In the words of John, "See how very much our heavenly Father loves us, for he allows us to be called his children—think of it—and we really *are!* But since most people don't know God, naturally they don't understand that we are his children" (1 John 3:1 TLB).

When we draw close to Jesus, we begin to spiritually resemble Him. And in heaven we will even have a glorified body like Jesus' body. But while we are on earth, we are to mature in Christ, because eternity's rewards will be permanent—not just an announcement on Judgment Day. We are to "become mature, attaining to the whole measure of the fullness of Christ" (Eph. 4:13), for heaven's rewards will be in perfect accord with the way we invested our lives here.

> No one can lay any foundation other than the one already laid, which is Jesus Christ. If any man builds on this foundation using gold, silver, costly stones, wood, hay or straw, his work will be shown for what it is, because the Day will bring it to light. It will be revealed with fire, and the fire will test the quality of each man's work. If what he has built survives, he will receive his reward. If it is burned up, he will suffer loss; he himself will be saved, but only as one escaping through the flames. (1 Cor. 3:11–15)

No, not everyone will receive the same eternal reward. That is why "each one should be careful how he builds" (v. 10). How much of our life—hours and days—will be burned up like straw and cause us to "suffer loss" in heaven? The Bible clearly warns us to consider this: "Those who are wise [who have wisely invested their hours and days] will shine like the brightness of the heavens, and those who lead many to righteousness, like the stars for ever and ever" (Dan. 12:3).

God delights to give us practical ways to express Christlikeness, to respond to people and to situations in a Jesus-like way. When heaven's angels observe us (and of course they always do—Ps. 91:11, Heb. 1:14), we might wonder whether they remark to each other, "Look, isn't that just like Jesus! They are really more and more like Jesus in their way of thinking about others and their way of responding to others. Can't you just see the love of Jesus in their thoughts and actions?"

The longer we lay our head on Jesus' breast in communing love, the more appropriately we should be able to reveal that love to others in our words and in the way we live with them. The church cannot avoid being greatly blessed when its members really commune with Jesus.

The witness of your life to unsaved people is also greatly strengthened and made more beautiful and clear as you live close to Jesus. The more closely we walk to Jesus' side, the more the unsaved world about us is reminded of Jesus and impacted for Him.

That is the way God has planned to use our lives. That is the way we shine as lights in the world (Phil. 2:15). Lights and stars are always beautiful. God loves light; He lives in glorious and beautiful light. (Heaven's light is like a crystal-clear jasper—Rev. 21:11).

As we by choice again and again deliberately seek to manifest to others Jesus' love, Jesus' loving care, Jesus' thoughtfulness, and Jesus' helpful concern, the angels record our life moment by moment in God's records (Ps. 56:8; Dan. 7:10; Mal. 3:16; Rev. 20:12). You are building your life on Jesus, the only foundation, and God is planning to reward each of your loving thoughts and prayers and words.

From the days of Abraham (Gen. 15:1–2) God has assured us that He will reward us. Keeping and meditating on God's Word bring great reward (Ps. 19:11). "He who sows righteousness reaps a sure reward" (Prov. 11:18). When God comes, He loves to bring rewards for the faithful (Isa. 40:10; 62:11). Jesus Himself loved to speak of heaven's rewards (Matt. 5:12) and was concerned lest those who belonged to Him failed to get the reward God their Father delighted to give (Matt. 6:1, 4, 6; 10:41–42; Luke 6:35). Even a cup of cold water given in Jesus' name will be rewarded (Mark 9:41).

In 1 Corinthians 3:8 we are assured "each will be rewarded according to his own labor." But Paul warns that if a Christian builds his life on Christ in a trivial way (wood, hay, or straw), God's fiery judgment will burn it up and "he will suffer loss" (v. 15). Saved—but with part of his life as a Christian burned up and a loss to him! How that disappoints the Father, who wants us to receive our full reward! John warns us, "Watch out that you do not lose what you have worked for, but that you may be rewarded fully" (2 John 8).

But how many are wasting their hours in watching television shows that do them no spiritual, moral, or educational good! How many spend much time reading books or periodicals for which God will not reward them, while the reward they could have received from prayer, spiritual reading, or being a blessing to others is forever lost. The reward God longed to give them they have forever forfeited.

They will be in heaven, but when they stand before Christ's judgment throne they will see the pain in His eyes. They will feel the regret that they failed to live more closely to Jesus, failed to share His heartbeat and concern for revival and missions, and invested so little time in praying for the church and Christ's kingdom. Saved, thank God! But so much of their life wasted. Saved, but so much of their life lived for self and lived as if God had not offered and promised rewards if we would qualify. Saved, but part of their life lost forever.

Will there be tears in heaven when people see how they lost the rewards the Triune God planned for them? I believe there will be many tears in heaven. But does not Scripture say that God will wipe away all tears? Yes, Thank God! But the last time that is said is after the final judgment.

Is God disappointed when we are so spiritually careless that we fail to go as fully from glory to glory as God has made it possible for us to do (2 Cor. 3:18)? Is He disappointed when we fail to obey, read His Word, or pray as He longs for us to do? Will

He be disappointed that we spent so little time in prayer that we failed to share with Jesus His burden for the salvation of the world, as He made it possible for us to do?

My heart repeats so often, and sometimes with tears, the familiar hymn we sang in church when I was a youth:

> Must Jesus bear the cross alone,
>> And all the world go free?
> No; there's a cross for everyone,
>> And there's a cross for me.

I want to bear a prayer burden for a lost world, don't you? I want to share tears with Jesus as I pray for missions, don't you? I want to invest prayer, tears, and deep longings for revival, which I know will occur in the Millennium, if not before. What a privilege to invest our lives here for eternity! How can we love Jesus less than to pour out our souls in prayer again and again for God's great final harvest?

The hymn continues:

> The consecrated cross I'll bear,
>> Till death shall set me free,
> And then go home my crown to wear,
>> For there's a crown for me.

> Upon the crystal pavement, down
>> At Jesus, piercéd feet,
> Joyful, I'll cast my golden crown,
>> And His dear name repeat.

> O precious cross! O glorious crown!
>> O resurrection day!
> Ye angels, from the stars come down,
>> And bear my soul away.

This is what God's glorious plan of salvation is all about. This is why Spirit-filled Christians have such a heart-hunger to be more and more like Jesus until we have the same heart-hunger as He in prayer, the same holy groanings in prayer for His kingdom to come and His will to be done. These yearnings prepare us to be part of that holy group of prayer warriors who over the centuries have prayed revivals into being and New Testament churches into existence.

We do not hunger for a beautiful crown. No! We hunger to share Jesus' love for the world, Jesus' prayer burden for the salvation of people. This hunger prepares our hearts to be more one with the heart of Jesus, our Great Intercessor, our enthroned High Priest (Heb. 7:17–8:1). He has in spiritual reality already seated us with Him on His high priestly throne (Eph. 2:6). We are to be reigning with Him already in priestly intercession as we share His heart burdens.

As you thus invest your life, Proverbs 4:18 will have its glorious and ultimate fulfillment: "The path of the righteous is like the first gleam of dawn, shining ever brighter till the full light of day." Or as Jesus said, "Then the righteous will shine like the sun in the kingdom of their Father" (Matt. 13:43).

Paul writes that "God knew his people in advance, and he chose them to become like his Son, so that his Son would be the firstborn, with many brothers and sisters" (Rom. 8:29 NLT), or in the words of the NIV, "Those God foreknew he also predestined to be conformed to the likeness of his Son." But when does this take place? When do we become like Jesus? Spiritually, we become like Him now, and then when He returns, we will be glorified in body and be visibly like Him. First John 3:2–3 in the *New Living Translation* says, "Yes, dear friends, we are already God's children, and we can't even imagine what we will be like when Christ returns. But we do know that when he comes we will be like him, for we will see him as he really is. And all who believe this will keep themselves pure, just as Christ is pure."

Will all true believers be like Jesus? Yes. Will heaven wipe out all differences of how clearly, obediently, and faithfully we have lived for Jesus here? Probably not. Will all receive the same heavenly rewards? Certainly not! Heaven's rewards are going to be gloriously different, specially designed by God for each individual. Not merely will there be distinguishing rewards in heaven; perhaps there will also be a difference in the shining "brightness" or beautiful glory, just as stars vary in their radiant beauty (1 Cor. 15:41).

Daniel associates spiritual wisdom and soul-winning with the brightness of our shining in heaven (Dan. 12:3). How must we be wise? The Hebrew word here for "wise" (*sākel*) gives the thought of insightful understanding and then acting prudently. "Do not be foolish [Gk. *aphron*—without reason or prudence], but understand what the Lord's will is" (Eph. 5:17). We must be wise in setting spiritual priorities, prudent in the investment of our life.

The preceding verses caution, "Be very careful, then, how you live—not as unwise but as wise, making the most of every opportunity" (vv. 15–16). This of course includes the investment of our intercessory prayer, as prayer partners with Jesus, as His royal intercessors (Eph. 2:6; 1 Peter 2:9; Rev. 1:5–6).

In summary, we are to become like Christ:

1. Building our lives on Jesus the one foundation, using those things and doing those things that in God's sight are gold and silver and not things that are straw and wood (1 Cor. 3:11).

2. Using our time and opportunities wisely. Before we become Christlike, worthy to be Christ's beloved bride, we need the following steps to transform us from being sinners into His holy likeness:

   a. Forgiveness of our sins and acceptance as a child of God.

   b. Cleansing of our sinful nature into a Spirit-cleansed holy nature (pure as He is pure, 1 John 3:3).

   c. Maturation of a life of spiritual wisdom and fruitfulness in soul-winning.

   d. Addition and cultivation of the fruit of the Spirit—a process the Spirit can greatly accelerate in our lives if we take the initiative to add to our spiritual life (2 Peter 1:5–7) but which need never end until we receive our glorified bodies in heaven.

Let us double-check to make sure that there is no sin in our lives (2 Peter 3:14). Then let us concentrate on the spiritual beauty and glory that God longs to cultivate in us here before we see Him face to face and on the effective prayer life of intercession He wishes to have us share today with Jesus, our holy Intercessor. One day we will share the crown He plans for His intercessors.

CHAPTER 19

Holy Love: The Ethic of the Spirit-Filled Life

What a godly life should be ours if God Himself indwells us! Peter asks in connection with Christ's return and the destruction of all material things, "What kind of people ought you to be? You ought to live holy and godly lives" (2 Peter 3:11).

When Paul speaks of Christ's judgment of Christians' works, he reminds us that Judgment Day will be a time when our works will be found to have been built either on that which lasts and survives the fire test or on that which is of no eternal benefit and is burned up (1 Cor. 3:15). Paul is not speaking of non-Christians but of those whose lives are built on the foundation of Jesus Christ (vv. 11–16). How much is found in Christian lives that is spiritually substandard! The judgment of God's fiery throne will prove much of what Christians do to be trivial, carnal, a waste of time.

What the Bible says about being saved and escaping hell could be contained in a very small volume. But page after page tells us how to live our lives worthily, with examples of those who did and those who did not. It gives both warnings and exhortations.

Every Scripture is God-breathed ... and profitable for instruction, for reproof *and* conviction of sin, for correction of error *and* discipline in obedience, [and] for training in righteousness (in holy living, in conformity to God's will in thought, purpose, and action), so that the man of God may be complete *and* proficient, well fitted *and* thoroughly equipped for every good work. (2 Tim. 3:16–17 AMP)

Thus, the goal of the Scriptures is to train people of God in holy living. Training takes time and involves instruction, watchfulness, and discipline. When the Holy Spirit indwells and fills us, He trains us to manifest His holiness. He shows us how to express His holy nature in our daily lives. The Holy Spirit does a radical work in the heart of the believer, bringing about a fundamental and thorough transformation. He expects the believer's life to be thereafter marked by His indwelling presence. The life of the Spirit-filled person should testify to the reality of the Holy Spirit and of God's work of grace in his or her soul.

The Bible uses drastic terminology for the work of entire sanctification—spiritual circumcision, or circumcision of the heart (Deut. 30:6). Sanctification enables believers to love God with all their heart—that is, to be filled with perfect love, which the Holy Spirit pours out (Rom. 5:5). True spiritual worship of God (Phil. 3:3) then becomes possible, since the sinful nature is thus put off "not with a circumcision done by the hands of men but with the circumcision done by Christ" (Col. 2:11).

Death to sin is termed being crucified with Christ (Gal. 2:20), because the sinful flesh has been crucified (5:24), enabling the Spirit-filled person to live and walk in the Spirit (v. 25). Thus, the old self (our carnal, sinful nature inherited from Adam) is crucified. Crucifixion does away with the body of sin (Rom. 6:6)—that is, sin in the singular, the sin nature from which the sins in one's life spring. Paul says the crucified person no longer serves sin or the sinful nature. The body is dead to sin (8:10), for the believer no longer lives according to the sinful nature (v. 5). This is the cleansing from all sin (singular) spoken of in 1 John 1:7.

Salvation is an instantaneous, radical work of the Spirit that takes place in the moment when the believer offers his or her life as a living sacrifice and the Spirit purifies the heart by faith and fills with His fullness. From that instant the person has victory over sin. God Himself does this great work in the soul, and He sanctifies "through and through," says Paul (1 Thess. 5:23). Now this holy life must be lived out daily.

The Spirit-filled life is not a life free from temptation. Holiness of heart does not exempt one from Satan's attacks. Perhaps temptations may be even more keen, for Christ, the sinless Son of God, was tempted more than any human being. Furthermore, He was tempted in every way, just as we are (Heb. 4:15). Sanctification frees from sin, but it does not free us from our personality or from our humanity with its possibility of sin. The forgetful person will still be forgetful; the dull person will still be slow to comprehend. The Spirit-filled person may misinterpret and misjudge, and mistakes will occur in spite of a heart filled with God-given love. The Holy Spirit purifies inner motives, but ethical action requires more than pure motives; it requires skill and tact in expression of pure love.

All ethical action requires three things. First, *it requires an understanding of the situation.* A sanctified, Spirit-filled person who fails to understand because of the human mind's limitations or inexperience may do the wrong thing just because he or she does not understand.

Second, *ethical action requires a pure motive.* When the Holy Spirit cleanses from all sin by applying the blood of Christ, He purifies our motives.

Third, *ethical action requires skill in practice.* Here is where we need the training to which Paul refers in 2 Timothy 3:16–17: "All Scripture is God-breathed and is useful for teaching, rebuking, correcting and training in righteousness, so that the man of God may be thoroughly equipped for every good work." The Holy Spirit uses the Bible as the textbook for training in holy living. How absolutely necessary that we fill our mind with God's Word (Ps. 119:11). Untrained persons can wound when they mean to bless, offend when they mean to help. Thus, we need the Spirit's guidance each day.

Because the world expects a high standard from Christians, it is imperative that Spirit-filled people express their holy love in a mature way. A Christian is like a city set upon a hill (Matt. 5:14). We cannot be hid. We should thank God that the world watches us, because this is our opportunity to bring glory to God. But too often non-Christians stumble because of what they see in professing Christians. The higher the testimony to the grace of God and the more saintliness the unsaved see in Spirit-filled Christians, the higher the standard they expect from all believers. Similarly, the higher the standard a Christian sets for other Christians to follow, the holier his or her own life must be. We dare not hinder our testimony and bring disparagement upon the work of the Spirit by inadequate ethical expression of our holy love.

The people of the world judge God and His salvation by what they see in us. They cannot see God's love pouring into our soul through the ministry of the Spirit. They can only see the way we express that love in our outward actions. They expect even higher standards from us than they require of themselves.

We dare not be blind to our faults but must humbly admit them. We dare not be careless in our words or crude in our actions. We dare not be tactless, for hungry, defeated people are watching us. If we manifest the fruit of the Spirit in our lives, many other hungry people will be attracted to Christ and God will be glorified.

Most important of all, God expects a very high standard of ethical living from us. He sent His Son to die for our cleansing. Christ gladly paid the price for our salvation—from both the guilt and the power of sin. And the Holy Spirit works within us, not merely to cleanse us, but to help us glorify Christ in all we say and do. We dare not grieve our holy triune God. Are we failing Him? How urgent it is that we constantly express the ethic of perfect, holy love in our relations with others.

Make My Life Your Witness

O Christ, will man prejudge Your claim
    By what he sees in me?
Will man reject or love Your name
    By my life's purity?
Am I Your letter to the lost?
Is Your seal on my life embossed?
Should I fail You, what tragic cost!
    Lord, help me Christlike be.

O Christ, does my unworthy life
    Witness to men clearly?
Do my own friends, my children, wife
    Christlikeness see in me?
Does Your pure beauty dress my soul?
Does Your Shekinah clothe the whole
Till men Your holiness extol
    From what they see in me?

O Christ, help me to really care
    And manifest Your grace.
May I Your holy image bear
    Upon my life and face.

May mine be e'er a Christlike touch;
I need Your graciousness so much
Till all my deeds and words are such
    That men Your glory trace.

May naught but holy ethics e'er
    In me be manifest.
May I Your constant fullness share
    As men put me to test.
My nature You did crucify;
Now may my whole life testify
To everyone who passes by
    Till they too seek Your best.

Wesley L. Duewel

When we look at our fellow Christians, we are in constant danger of misjudging their ethics. We must always remember that we see only their actions, never their heart. God, however, looks on the heart. We must be holy ourselves but charitable with the actions of others. If it has taken God so long to train us how to express His grace, how patient we should be with others.

It is true that an ethical problem is a moral problem, and sin and holiness are moral issues. But we must remember that there are two aspects to judging every action, a moral and a nonmoral one. Motivation is always the moral aspect. But the application of the motivating principle always involves nonmoral aspects. Here is where it is so easy to misjudge.

Scripture says that a sinful motive brings the same guilt as the sinful act. For example, adultery can be committed in one's heart (Matt. 5:28), and hate is murder in God's sight (1 John 3:15). Only God can judge our motives. When the Holy Spirit fills and sanctifies us, He cleanses us of all impure motives.

We begin to judge when we see an action, and because we cannot see the motive, we can easily misjudge. One's motive may be pure, but because of forgetfulness, illogical reasoning, misunderstanding of a situation or another person, or a lack of communication skills, the pure motive may be expressed in an unfortunate way. Thus, we must be charitable with others, even as we want them to be charitable with us.

Perhaps a Spirit-filled person is so lost in thought about a problem in his home that he fails to notice a friend he passes on the street. The other person may think he is avoiding him and does not love him even though the troubled man may have a heart overflowing with love for the one he seemed to ignore. Or perhaps a Spirit-filled woman has been given wrong information about a believer. She believes the false information and suspects her sister and doubts that she is living victoriously. Then perhaps on that very day, the Christian she doubts is crushed by an attack of Satan until she can hardly lift her voice in prayer during a prayer meeting. The person given the false information may think this proves that something is wrong in the other woman's life and that guilt keeps her from praying. How often we would praise the person we blame if we could only see as God sees.

Furthermore, believers may agree on a major moral principle yet disagree when trying to work out specific details for applying that principle. Beware lest you condemn the convictions of others that spring from their pure hearts. Judge not that you be not judged (Matt. 7:1–2). Romans 14:1–4 instructs us in these points:

1. You must accept people even though their convictions differ from yours.
2. You must not despise the convictions of other believers.
3. God is the judge, not you.
4. You yourself will be judged by Christ for how you judge others.

God has led you step by step in understanding His Word and in manifesting His life. You must be as patient with others as God has been with you.

The heart of the Spirit-filled person is filled with holy love. We must express this love to others and be charitable in interpreting their love. The more the Spirit works within you, the more God's love will be manifest through you. Love always acts.

Love Always Acts

You cannot hide a burning love;
It triumphs obstacles above.
Love shows itself upon the face;
It adds a touch of lovely grace.
It puts a gleam within the eye,
Love proves itself; it cannot lie.
Love always shows!

A burning love you can't restrain;
It gives itself time and again.
    It seeks for ways in which to serve;
    For sacrifice it strengthens nerve.
It finds a thousand ways to please,
Forgetting its own will and ease.
    Love always gives!

Where burning love is really fact
It recognizes ways to act.
    It does not hesitate or wait;
    In serving, love is never late.
Love proves its presence every day;
It brings all else within its sway.
    Love always acts!

And he who loves Christ more than all
Will prove it in ways great and small.
    In all that he may do or say,
    His love will show itself each day.
His life will manifest God's grace
And love for Christ will light his face—
    For God is love!

Wesley L. Duewel

The love of the Spirit-filled person is true love, the love of 1 Corinthians 13. It knows no jealousy, envy, pride, covetousness, or ill will. When we are filled with God, we are filled with love, for God is love (1 John 4:8). Although we will never be perfect in mind or body as Adam was perfect, we can be perfect in love, for God purifies our love (1 John 4:17–18). Our love will not be infinite, but it will increase as we follow the Holy Spirit's guidance and discipline.

Only as we exercise God's redeeming love in sharing Christ with others will we remain Spirit-filled. We must, with Christ, share Calvary love with a missionary passion. Redemptive love feels a sense of responsibility for the salvation of others that begins with our next-door neighbors (our own Jerusalem—Acts 1:8) and extends to the ends of the earth.

Redemptive love is not based on the worthiness of the recipient. It reaches out to the most degraded as well as to the most educated and cultured; it loves those whose lives are most promising and those whose lives seem hopeless. No person can love soul-winning as much as a Spirit-filled person, for concern for the salvation of others is born of the Holy Spirit. Christians who close their hearts to others' needs are in danger of losing the fullness of the Spirit.

Redemptive love works in practical ways to resolve crises, to restore broken relationships, and to bring out the most effective service from others. Spirit-filled persons feel indebted to bring every unsaved person to the transforming love of Christ and to serve their fellow Christians. Redemptive love causes them to desire to meet every need as far as possible. Such love is unselfish, flexible, humble, and constantly seeking to serve others. It is the kind of love that causes one to put on an apron and wash others' feet (John 13:4–5, 15). We Christians love because God first loved us (1 John 4:1–9) and because He continues to love through us.

This is the ethic of the Spirit-filled life—holy, self-giving, redemptive love. All of the other fruit of the Spirit grow from it (Gal. 5:22–23), and it increases as we hunger and ask God for more, for if we ask, we will receive (Luke 11:13). By this combination—constant hunger for more of the Spirit, continual transfiguration by the Spirit into the glorious likeness of Jesus Christ, and steadfast guidance and discipline of the Spirit to enable us to express the life of the Spirit that indwells us—we will be a center of revival and blessing to God's cause wherever we are, and others will see and hunger to know God too.

CHAPTER 20

Are You Filled with the Spirit?

Are you filled with the Spirit? Jesus' purpose in dying on Calvary was to make you holy. "Jesus . . . suffered outside the city gate to make the people holy through his own blood. Let us, then, go to him outside the camp, bearing the disgrace he bore" (Heb. 13:12–13). Stopping short of a Spirit-filled life deprives Christ of the holy satisfaction of fulfilling His supreme purpose for your life.

Christ wants to cleanse you by His blood from all sin (1 John 1:7, 9) and also wants to save you from willful sinning (1 John 3:6, 9) and make your will one with His. Christ's desire is to make you pure and holy in this life, "to enable [you] to serve him without fear in holiness and righteousness . . . all [your] days" (Luke 1:74–75).

Christ is counting on your being part of His radiantly beautiful bride, His church. "Christ loved the church and gave himself up for her to make her holy, cleansing her by the washing with water through the word, and to present her to himself as a radiant church, without stain or wrinkle or any other blemish, but holy and blameless" (Eph. 5:25–27).

He wants to cleanse you now so that you will never be an embarrassment to Him as His bride. He wants to display you before all the angels of heaven and introduce you to His Father. He wants your Holy Spirit-filled life of love to teach the angels more about His salvation and grace as they watch you now (Eph. 3:10–11). His ultimate purpose for all eternity is that you be in the closest relationship of love as His bride. No angel will ever become as precious to Christ as you.

You are unworthy in your own merits to be Christ's bride, but He died to make you worthy. Christ not only wants to cleanse you and fill you with His Spirit, but He wants you to be transfigured until you bear His holy likeness, even as He bears the image of the Father. "Where the Spirit of the Lord is, there is freedom. And we, who with unveiled faces all reflect the Lord's glory, are being transformed into his likeness with ever-increasing glory, which comes from the Lord, who is the Spirit" (2 Cor. 3:17–18).

If you are already rejoicing in the preciousness of the Spirit-filled life, make it your joy, your constant hunger and prayer, to be ever more transfigured into His likeness. How can you measure your progress? Measure it by the depth and constancy of your desire for more of His likeness. Measure it by your prayer partnership with Jesus as you intercede for souls, His kingdom, and revival. Measure it by your openness to His guidance and your obedience to His will.

Peterson paraphrases 2 Corinthians 3:18 in *The Message*: ". . . nothing between us and God, our faces shining with the brightness of his face. And so we are transfigured much like the Messiah, our lives gradually becoming brighter and more beautiful as God enters our lives and we become like him." What blessed, beautiful provision God has made for us! He wants us as His bride to be blessedly like Him in holy beauty and in glory. He wants to begin transfiguring us now, and then at the resurrection He plans to glorify our bodies so that we will share His beautiful likeness for all eternity. Imagine having a face-to-face relationship with Christ for all eternity, His heart's love flowing through yours as His bride!

"Dear friends, now we are the children of God, and what we will be has not yet been made known. But we know that when he appears, we shall be like him, for we shall see him as he is. Everyone who has this hope in him purifies himself, just as he is pure" (1 John 3:2–3). Do you realize what Jesus is saying? You will be "like Jesus." No angel will ever mistake you for a fellow angel, because you will be too much like Jesus to be mistaken for an angel. In indescribable, sacred ways you will be like Jesus.

You will experience Jesus' holy and infinite love in a very delightfully blessed and infinitely personal way, for you are personally important to Him. He will have the record of all your responses to Him—your love, your obedience in drawing close to Him, your prayer communion with Him, and your intercessory partnership with Him as you prevailed in prayer and wept for the needs of the world and those about you. You are not just a computer number to Jesus. You will never be lost in the crowd. Just as He has gloriously personalized His relations with you up until now, He will continue to do so forever. He is joyously awaiting you and has glorious plans for you throughout eternity.

Revelation 19:7 assures us that at the wedding supper of the Lamb, the bride will have made herself ready for Jesus. That is what you are doing now as the Holy Spirit fills and transfigures you. The more you love and worship Him, the more closely you will be bound to Him and He to you. The more you are transfigured into His likeness now, the more thrilled Jesus is as He prepares for your eternity with Him.

Therefore, let us like Paul have one constant endeavor—to know Christ better and to be transfigured into His likeness. "Whatever was to my profit I now consider loss for the sake of Christ. What is more, I consider everything a loss compared to the surpassing greatness of knowing Christ Jesus my Lord. . . . I want to know Christ. . . . One thing I do: Forgetting what is behind and straining toward what is ahead, I press on toward the goal to win the prize for which God has called me heavenward in Christ Jesus" (Phil. 3:7–14).

If you have not yet found the glorious blessedness of being filled with the Spirit, if you have not proved it real in your own daily living, you can enter a new day of purity and power, a new day of communion with and service for God. You can know in your daily experience what it means to be filled with the Spirit, what it is like to hunger for more of His presence and power, what it is like to obey Jesus to the full. You can begin the glorious transfiguration process, which will not be completed until you stand at Jesus' feet, changed into His likeness, thrilling to eternity's rewards. Will you be filled with His Spirit?

Come, Oh Come, We Plead

Blessed Holy Spirit, come again today;
Come, indwell us fully in a mighty way.
    We are longing, waiting for Your grace and pow'r;
    Blessed Holy Spirit, come on us this hour!

Chorus:
Come upon us now! Come upon us now!
Hungry, thirsty, longing, we before You bow.
    Work in all Your fullness in and through us all;
    Hungry and obeying, Lord, in faith we call.

Blessed Holy Spirit, let Shekinah fall;
May Your holy glory come upon us all.
    May Your fire and glory now on us descend;
    Put Your seal upon us; then in service send.

Blessed Holy Spirit, work so all can see;
Exercise Your lordship—all Your ministry.
    Work in pow'r more fully than we've seen or heard;
    'Tis Your blessed promise, 'tis Your holy Word.

Blessed Holy Spirit, oh, do not delay!
Come in might and glory; come on us today!
    'Tis for You we hunger; it is You we need!
    Blessed Holy Spirit, come, oh come! we plead.

Wesley L. Duewel

Prayer of Love and Longing

Please join me in this prayer:

Blessed, wonderful, glorious Lord Jesus, You are the Son of God from all eternity, but You loved us so much that You left heaven with all its glories and became the Son of Man. You endured our sinful world, suffering the rejection, hatred, and evil of men. You took upon Yourself human life from babyhood to death—and, oh, what a cruel death! You did it all because of Your infinite, personal love.

You loved us even before the world was created. You chose us and longed for us even before You created Adam and Eve to be our foreparents. You loved us to the uttermost as you lived for us, prayed for us, and wept for us in Gethsemane. In Your agonizing love, You sweated drops of blood. Your heart was broken for us on the cross, and still You love us and long for us.

You understand me better than I understand myself. You know my every thought, desire, and weakness, yet You love me. You are longing and waiting for me to spend eternity with You as part of the special group You are preparing to be Your bride. You want me to be close to You in Your home, at Your side, seeing Your face, closer to You even than any of the angels of heaven!

Jesus, I love You, I worship You, I adore You. Thank You for saving me from my sins. Thank You that not one of my sins that You have forgiven will ever be remembered against me again. Thank You that although You hated my sin, You loved me so much that You died for me. Thank You that You realized how polluted, enslaved, and sinful my human nature was—incurable until You cleansed me. You were grieved over my sinfulness, envy, jealousy, stubbornness, anger, pride, deceitfulness, and hatred. Thank You that You not only bore on Calvary all the committed sins of humankind, but that You also bore all the sinfulness and unholiness of our nature. Thank You that not only did You take away all of our sins but that You also provided Your precious blood to cleanse us from the inner sin of our nature. Thank You, wonderful, infinitely loving Jesus. Thank You for cleansing me.

And thank You that You have given me grace upon grace and made it possible for me to grow more like You in personality and character. Thank You that the Holy Spirit was not through with me when He regenerated me or even when He cleansed my nature and filled me with Himself, but thank You that He joyfully labors to transfigure me into all the beauty that fills You, my beloved Jesus.

Loving Jesus, You are glorious beyond the ability of my words to describe, yet You long for me to be more like You. Clothe me with more of Your beauty—Your love, humility, patience, joy, and peace. Transfigure me from one degree of Your glory to another.

Let Your beauty, Lord Jesus, be seen in me,
All Your Christlikeness, glory and purity.
Oh, my Savior divine, my whole being refine,
Until Your beauty, Lord Jesus, be seen in me.

I thank You that as You take me into Your presence in heaven, You will glorify even my body, giving me a body more like Yours than I have ever dreamed possible. Oh, Jesus, I shall at last be transfigured body, soul, and spirit forever!

O that will be glory for me, glory for me, glory for me;
When by Your grace I shall look on Your face,
That will be glory, be glory for me.

In Jesus' glorious name. Amen.

HOLY LOVE

1 Corinthians 13 in the Words
of Various Translations and Paraphrases

I have combined words and phrases from various New Testament translations and paraphrases of the fifteen beautiful descriptive statements in 1 Corinthians 13 to help us better comprehend the high spiritual standard set by God for those He fills with His Spirit. Let us not despair of ever reaching this standard of holiness of character, but let us thank God that He wills it for us and reach out in prayer and faith to make it our own.

1. Holy love is forbearing, longsuffering, very patient. Love never gives up.
2. Holy love is very kind. Love cares more for others than for self; it is gracious, gentle, benign. It mellows all that would have been harsh, severe.
3. Holy love is never jealous; it does not envy.
4. Holy love does not boast or brag; it does not parade itself or strut. It does not seek to display itself or show itself off.
5. Holy love is not proud, is not puffed up, is not conceited, is not ostentatious or arrogant, does not have an inflated ego or act unbecomingly or unmannerly, is not graceless.
6. Holy love is not selfish or self-seeking. It does not demand its own way or want "me first." It does not insist on its own rights.
7. Holy love is not irritable, does not fly off the handle, is not quick tempered or quick to take offense. Holy love is not touchy, fretful, or resentful.

8. Holy love keeps no record of wrongs, no score of wrongs, pays no attention to a suffered wrong, does not remember wrongs done against it. Holy love will hardly even notice when others do it wrong; it bears no malice.

9. Holy love never rejoices over wrongdoing or injustice. It does not revel when others grovel, nor does it gloat over other people's sins.

10. Holy love delights in truth, joyfully sides with the truth, rejoices whenever truth wins out.

11. Holy love puts up with anything, covers up everything. It knows how to be silent. Love is always supportive, is always ready to excuse; it bears up under anything and everything that comes. Holy love patiently accepts all things, endures all things, and can overlook faults.

12. Holy love trusts God always, can stand any kind of treatment, and believes all things. Holy love is always trustful, has unquenchable faith, is always eager to believe the best, is always supportive, loyal.

13. Holy love is always hopeful. It hopes under all circumstances, it keeps up hope in everything. Holy love never regards anything or anyone as hopeless; it always looks for the best.

14. Holy love does not lose heart or courage; it is full of endurance. It endures without limit. It gives us power to endure everything; it always continues strong. Holy love endures everything without weakening. It never looks back.

15. Holy love never fails or comes to an end. It never fades out or becomes obsolete. Holy love lasts forever. It keeps going to the end.

Lord, perfect this love in me. Flood me with more and more of this, Your holy love. Amen.

NOTES

Chapter 3: The Word Pictures God Uses

1. *The Works of Wesley,* Journals, Dec. 31, 1760–Sept. 13, 1773, 3:54.

2. Ibid., "Of Christian Perfection," 11:508.

Chapter 9: Spirit-Filled Examples

1. V. Raymond Edman, *They Found the Secret* (Grand Rapids: Zondervan, 1984), 18.

2. Ibid., 20.

3. Ibid., 20–23.

4. Ibid., 43–45.

5. Ibid., 45.

6. R. A. Torrey, *Why God Used D. L. Moody* (Chicago: Moody Bible Institute Press, 1923), 57.

7. Ibid., 57–58.

8. Ibid., 60–63.

9. D. W. Lambert, *Oswald Chambers: An Unbribed Soul* (Fort Washington, Pa.: Christian Literature Crusade, 1983), 23–24.

10. Ibid., 60–61.

11. Bertha Chambers, *Oswald Chambers: His Life and Work* (London: Simpkin Marshall Ltd., 1938), 77.

12. Ibid., 158.

13. Ibid.

14. Ibid., 202.

15. Ibid., 236.

16. Ibid., 251.

Chapter 13: Transfiguring Growth: Our Responsibility

1. Henry Joseph Thayer, *Greek-English Lexicon of the New Testament* (New York: Harper & Brothers, 1889), 661.

2. See Matthew 6:6; 10:41–42; 16:27; 1 Corinthians 3:8; Galatians 6:8–9; Colossians 3:23–24; Hebrews 11:26; 2 John 8; Revelation 11:18.

Chapter 14: Radiant Lives and Faces

1. James Gilchrist Lawson, *Deeper Experiences of Famous Christians* (Anderson, Ind.: Warner Press, 1911), 84.

2. Clara McLeister, *Men and Women of Deep Piety* (Cincinnati: God's Bible School and Revivalist, 1920), 511.

3. Lawson, *Deeper Experiences*, 198–99.

4. Ibid., 255.

5. Rosalind Goforth, *Goforth of China* (Grand Rapids: Zondervan, 1937), 361.

6. Ibid., 351.

7. Ibid., 38.

8. Ibid., 363.

9. Ibid., 91.

10. Ibid., 347–48.

11. Andrew Woolsey, *Duncan Campbell—A Biography* (London: Hodder and Stoughton, 1974), 94.

12. Ibid., 181–82.

13. John Shearer, *Old Time Revivals* (London: Pickering & Inglis, n.d.), 76.

14. Ibid., 77.

15. D. Martyn Lloyd-Jones, *Revival* (Westchester, Ill.: Crossway, 1987), 206.

Chapter 16: Shekinah Glory upon the Spirit-Filled

1. Andrew Woolsey, *Duncan Campbell—A Biography* (London: Hodder and Stoughton, 1974), 173.

2. Ibid., 180.

3. Basil Miller, *Praying Hyde: A Man of Prayer* (Grand Rapids: Zondervan, 1943), 125.

INDEX OF POEMS

OTHER BOOKS BY DR. DUEWEL

Touch the World Through Prayer. A challenging, very readable manual on prayer that has been used by God to revitalize the prayer life of thousands. A Christian best-seller.

Let God Guide You Daily. A manual on guidance to help you enter into the joy of God's guidance as the daily experience of your life.

Ablaze for God. A book to challenge all Christians, especially Christian workers and lay leaders, to a life and service that are Spirit-filled, Spirit-empowered, and mightily used by God.

Mighty Prevailing Prayer. Let the Spirit use this powerful volume to make your intercession mighty before God. A guide to intensified intercession and prayer warfare.

Measure Your Life. Seventeen ways God is measuring your life as He prepares for your eternal reward.

Revival Fire. The thrilling account of God's mighty working in major revivals in many parts of the world, especially during the last three centuries.

God's Power Is for You. Grow deeper in your relationship with Jesus by thinking about all the ways He touches our lives and how we can become more devoted to Him. More than fifty meditations give insight into prayer, obedience, spirituality, and faithfulness.

One or more of Dr. Duewel's books have been published in forty-nine languages or national editions. Some one million of his books are already in circulation. English editions of all available from Christian bookstores or the author.

Duewel Literature Trust, Inc.
740A Kilbourne Drive
Greenwood, IN 46142–1843

If God has made this book a blessing to you and you wish to share your testimony, or if you wish the author to remember you in a moment of prayer, feel free to write:

Dr. Wesley L. Duewel
P.O. Box A
Greenwood, IN 46142–6599

Mighty Prevailing Prayer

by Wesley Duewel

Softcover 0-310-36191-5

God has a more effective prayer life for you than you ever dreamed possible. Let this volume be your open door to wonderful answers to prayer. Here is your personal guide to a life of mighty prevailing prayer.

This book will speak to your heart, take you to your knees, and help you obtain prayer answers for even difficult and resistant situations. Leonard Ravenhill calls it an "encyclopedia." You will want to read and refer to it again and again. It is a lifetime investment.